Forgiveness

How Religion Endangers Morality

R.A. Sharpe

imprint-academic.com

Published in the UK by
Imprint Academic, PO Box 200, Exeter EX5 5YX, UK

Published in the USA by
Imprint Academic, Philosophy Documentation Center
PO Box 7147, Charlottesville, VA 22906-7147, USA

ISBN-13: 978184540 083 5

A CIP catalogue record for this book is available from the
British Library and US Library of Congress

Front Cover Caption:

RAMALLAH, WEST BANK – NOV. 14, 2000
A Palestinian youth uses a sling to throw stones
at Israeli soldiers during a clash in Ramallah.

Photograph © Jock Fistick 2000

Contents

Preface

Bob Sharpe is perhaps best known as an aesthetician and a life-long passion for music provided the inspiration for much of his writing. But in a philosophical career spanning almost fifty years he also taught, and published work on, subjects ranging from science and logic to psychology and ethics.

The Moral Case Against Religious Belief (1997) grew out of our years of discussion of the subject and its publication was followed by a realisation that there was more to be said and a sequel needed. *Forgiveness* is that sequel, on which Bob was working until his sudden fatal illness. Although at that time he did not consider the book finished, he was undecided as to what more he wanted to say. Accordingly, rather than add any new material, I have edited his typescript and hand-written notes and combined them to produce this book. I ask readers to bear in mind that the result may not be quite what he would have published himself.

I am indebted to Anthony Freeman and the staff of Imprint Academic for their advice and support, to Andrew Gleeson, who kindly provided me with details of his correspondence with Bob on the subject of forgiveness, and to David Cockburn for his unfailing encouragement and constructive criticism. Thanks too, for useful comments and discussion, to students, staff and friends at University of Wales, Lampeter, where both Bob and I read papers based on sections of this book.

Lynne Sharpe
June 2007

Chapter One

Introduction

Tantum religio potuit suadere malorum
So great is the power of religion to lead us to evil.[1]

If Lucretius could write this in a polytheistic culture which, if Nietzsche is to be believed, tends to be more tolerant, what would one say of monotheistic religions today? When, in 1997, I published a book entitled *The Moral Case against Religious Belief*, a member of the audience at the launch remarked that I had been kind to believers. I did indeed try to be generous, partly because I owed much to a Christian upbringing, a large part of which I still valued. I also appreciated just how much religion was part of an identity which should not, indeed could not, be discarded at the behest of a philosopher, even if his arguments were cogent. I was then, and am still, a post-Christian.

The intervening decade has brought home to us the terrible results of religious conviction. It is the festering sore of the Israeli-Palestinian conflict more than any other factor that is responsible for the desperate state of international relations in the Middle East. Any attempt to suggest in the British Press that Israel is primarily responsible for this receives a prompt and furious reply from a Zionist. (The fault is perhaps more to be laid at the feet of the Balfour Declaration and the Nazi years in central Europe). Nevertheless, religion is at the root of this. On the television news recently, a young Israeli was being questioned about the Israeli occupation in Gaza. He explained that God had given the land to the Jews and added, and these were his words, 'End of story'. Now I do not want to concern myself

---

[1]   Lucretius 1.101.

here with whether it is plausible to suppose that a minor mountain deity from a pantheon of Near Eastern Gods worshipped three millennia ago happened to be the only one of that ilk who really existed, the others being mythical, or whether He alone survived whilst the rest of them died out (of laughter at the preposterous claim to uniqueness, if Nietzsche is to be believed). Nor do I want to question whether His land grants to the tribes of Israel are accurately reported. As you will probably have guessed, to say that I find all this implausible understates the matter.

What I do want to point out is the connection with a problem which goes back to the ancient Greeks, known as the Euthyphro dilemma. When the Gods say something is good is it because it is really good or is it good because the Gods say it is? If the Gods said something which we thought to be bad was really good would that make it good? Is it conceivable that forced expropriation of land is really just — though not 'justice as we know it'? I wanted to say to the young Israeli, 'But look here, these people have been living in this land for generations; you have just arrived from Australia; how can it be right to take their land, their water supplies, their olive-groves, away from them by force? It cannot be right any more than it would be right for my fellow Cornishmen to march into Devon and take the land away from Devonians by force, simply because their ancestors lived there before the Anglo-Saxon invasion.' Suppose I accept his answer, that God granted them the land three millennia ago, how would that change things? Suppose it was all true and that God did say this and did not change his mind when he realised that a hasty judgement born out of sympathy for the Jews in captivity was going to lead to disastrous consequences later on. Then, I suggest, we ought to conclude that such a God ought not to be obeyed on this matter and, furthermore, that any God capable of such a catastrophic error of moral judgement certainly ought not to be worshipped. 'End of story', as the young Israeli said.

We might wish it was the end of the story regardless of whether the young Israeli is correct or not. But, of course, it is not the end. We have experienced violence upon violence.

President Bush's assaults are backed by a Christian Right which seems to have a very tender conscience over aborted foetuses but very little conscience over the detention without trial, and the torture, of prisoners of war in contravention of the Geneva Conventions, nor any great concern that the death penalty in the USA is routinely applied to the innocent and mentally ill, nor any concern in allying with regimes which practise torture, as long as they are welcoming to American business concerns. I view the growing influence of religion in politics with fear and horror. As a distinguished Christian thinker said at a lecture at which I was present a few years ago, if mankind is to perish religion may very well be the cause.

In the light of all this, it is astonishing that religion is so often defended on the basis that religious belief is the answer to relativism in morality — that religion 'guarantees' morality in some way or another such that the dreaded relativism cannot take hold. 'Relativism' usually goes unexplained. The idea seems to be that for the relativist there is no way to choose between rival moral schemes. The morality of somebody who thinks that you should forgive your enemies cannot be shown to be preferable to the morality of somebody who thinks that you should pay them back in like coin. However much you might find the morality of the selfish materialist reprehensible, the fact is that you cannot show her to be wrong. In the light of fundamental moral disputes of this sort, you simply hold up your hands. This is relativism and, in the language of the religious believer, it is frequently associated with materialism.

Now, of course, there is no reason why a relativist should be a shallow materialist in the sense that consumer goods are all that he is interested in and cares about. He may well be concerned about injustice, inequality and poverty. But, it seems, all that he can do in the face of those who are not concerned is to retire from the fray. He has no way of convincing them that they are wrong because, in the end, arguments run out. There are no facts with which he can confront them. But even if this is so, the relativist is not morally objectionable on these grounds. He may very well regret his impotence here.

It may be the case that there are no independent grounds to which we can appeal to show that the values of the Vikings or the Ancient Romans were wrong and that ours are right. Certainly religion could not provide these grounds. There are two reasons for this. Consider this first. Islam and Christianity are religions of the book. But there is no independent basis on which you can persuade a Moslem that the Bible is the word of God and that the Koran is not or persuade the Christian that the Koran is the word of God and the Bible is not. Whilst writing this, I heard an orthodox Rabbi declare that the Torah was dictated by God to Moses, adding without irony that no human intelligence was involved. Most religious believers of other faiths would reject this. So how do we decide between competing claims as to the Word of God? We cannot. Neither can it be shown that the creed of one religion is right and the other wrong. As a reply to relativism the appeal to religion simply shifts the argument one stage back; we are still left with opposed views; there are no independent grounds for choosing between them. Whatever arguments are produced for or against will be met by various forms of casuistry. The claims of religion are not obviously true; they are not self-evident. Mostly they are obviously false. So how could they provide a basis for morality? If we are told 'God says you must spare your enemies' on the one hand and 'God says you must kill infidels' on the other, how are we to choose between them , given that at some point they will conflict?

Secondly, just suppose that one or the other religion is true; why should I act upon it? It is possible, is it not, that God might order me to do something and I might refuse because it is wicked? If God ordered me not to use contraception then I may well have a moral case for disobeying him. Enter the Euthyphro dilemma once more.

Now one plausible answer to the Euthyphro dilemma is this. The conception of God which operates amongst believers is one which normally, though not inevitably, enshrines the moral concepts the believer accepts. Tell me that God says I should extirpate my unbelieving neighbour and I will say that God cannot possibly demand such a thing. It is incompatible with his nature—and I say that because I invest God's nature with the values I myself endorse. The problem is that this does nothing at all for the attempt to prosecute relativism. As moralities differ so will conceptions of God. Some believers think they should kill people who insult their religion. Others do not. Different conceptions of God and what he requires of us morally, remain and we cannot appeal to any independent basis to justify one or the other.

I conclude that the claims of religion to answer the problems raised by relativism are entirely bogus.

II

I have spoken as though relativism is a potent objection to the moral certitudes of believers. Am I allowing that the arguments of the relativists are so powerful that they cannot be gainsaid? Matters are more complicated. We need to make distinctions. It is something of a cliché amongst many philosophers that two people can agree, say, that Eichmann ordered the killing of children but that one might say that it is wrong whereas the other might say that it is justified because these are Jewish children. Colin McGinn, echoing the views of other philosophers such as Williams and Harman, remarks that whereas facts about the world cause our beliefs in them, moral facts do not cause our moral beliefs. If there are moral facts, then, unlike 'scientific facts', they are causally inert. As McGinn puts it, ethical belief is not explained by ethical facts in the way scientific beliefs are explained by scientific facts.[2]

For a start, talk of 'belief' here is odd. I do not 'believe' that tables have a molecular structure; I know it just as I know there is a large oak tree in the field below our house. To talk of belief here suggests that I think I might be wrong. But in many cases I do not think that I might be wrong. I do not

---

[2]   Colin McGinn, *Ethics, Evil and Fiction* (Oxford University Press, 1997), p. 36.

think I might be wrong in my view that torture is an abomi-
nation and should never be practised. Do you want to insist
that I also believe these things as well as knowing them? Go
ahead, if you must, but your insistence is something I
acknowledge with irritation. You are only making this
demand because you are driven by a philosophical theory.
It is a tendentious misdescription much as it would be if, in
court, I were to be asked if I knew the woman in the dock
when, in fact, she is my wife. Of course I know her.

Moral beliefs and moral facts? Well, it is not a belief that I
should not pass by the injured and frightened toddler if neither of his parents are in view. I know I should not do this.
You press me on 'moral facts'. Why should I not say that his
injury is a moral fact which causes my moral belief that I
should aid him? If you want to talk about scientific facts
causing scientific beliefs, I see no reason why you should
not grant that there are moral facts which cause moral
beliefs even though a greater care for the nuances of English
would require that moral facts cause moral *knowledge*. Of
course, we might re-describe the toddler in terms of body A
impacting on surface B and then what we have is a 'scientific fact'. But there is no reason at all to suppose that this
description is 'closer to reality' or 'more basic'. After all, this
is not a meteorite impacting on the earth's surface, it is a
human child and the 'more basic' description distorts. It
leaves out what is important. Indeed, to describe the 'facts'
in this way displays a sort of moral coarseness. One can be a
realist about some values and remain a pluralist about the
bulk of values and this is how it is. So it is not only monists
(who believe in a single over-riding scheme of values) who
can be realists.

I do not deny that there are complex cases where there is
no clear answer or perhaps no single answer at all as to what
to do. To abort a foetus may sometimes be such a problem
case; there will be cases where it is clearly right, where the
foetus is a few hours old and the mother is the victim of
rape; no question of killing a human being is involved here
because a few cells are not a human being. (The claim that it
is is tendentious nonsense which denies the obvious for

religious motives.) It seems to me clearly wrong to abort a six-month-old foetus merely because the parents want to go on holiday.[3] In the same way there are complex 'factual' judgements where the evidence has to be weighed up. Whether or not the dinosaurs died out as a result of an asteroid impact now looks to be a far more complex issue than we once thought. But that does not mean that there are not straight forward facts such as that I am now typing at a PC; to deny this would suggest madness, ignorance of the language, or suggest that the speaker has been perverted by philosophy or perhaps religion. If relativism denies that there are straight forward moral cases where there is no room for doubt, then the relativist is mistaken. Torturing infants for fun is obviously wrong. Of that I am as certain as I am that a PC is currently a foot or so from my face.

Indeed the considerations which lead to the denial of the obvious in both moral and factual contexts do not seem that different one from the other. The delusions of religion cause somebody to believe, against the reports of common sense over generations, that a stone statue of the Virgin nods at him. Currently (July 2005) a statue of the Virgin in Naples is said to be kicking her legs at the audience. The reports of uneducated peasant girls in Portugal that the Virgin appeared to them and told them a few things are believed contrary to the known facts that such apparitions are delusions. (I wonder why the Virgin did not tell them something really useful such as the recipe for penicillin. Still I should, in fairness, concede that the deliverances of spiritual encounters are not always completely useless. The first vision of the mystic Swedenborg occurred when he was eating a meal in a tavern in Bishopsgate Street, London, gobbling his food as was his wont. Jesus appeared in a corner of the dining room and offered the sage advice 'Eat more slowly'.)[4] Equally, obvious moral considerations can be

---

[3]   See the excellent study of this topic by Rosalind Hursthouse, *Beginning Lives* (Blackwell, 1987).

[4]   The anecdote seems to have come via Thomas Carlyle. See the diary entry of Caroline Fox for June 5th 1842 quoted in Irene and Allan Taylor eds., *The Assassin's Cloak* (Canongate, 2000).

denied or ignored. So something similar to the refusal to deny the obvious – that visions are delusions which occur to the unstable, the foolish, to children or to people who are mesmerised by a religion or an ideology – allows a man to murder a child simply because he is a Jew.[5]

Different religions appear, at least to some extent, to value different things. A universal religion which contained the lowest common denominator of the popular religions, such as Islam or Christianity, would not contain very much. Isaiah Berlin famously alerted us to the incommensurability of values. Speaking of reading Machiavelli, he observes 'The idea that this planted in my mind was the realisation, which came as something of a shock, that not all the supreme values pursued by mankind now and in the past were necessarily compatible with one another.'[6] To this misconception he ascribed much of the misery that mankind inflicts upon itself. Now in one way it may seem obvious that we differ in what we value. One man spends his spare time playing chess, a game which does not interest me, though I can easily imagine that it might have. A woman collects Coronation Mugs or teapots, a hobby which I simply cannot imagine pursuing. Another is absorbed by classical music which means nothing to somebody else and so on. In all these cases, we are not bothered by the fact that somebody else values an object which, to us, seems worthless or pursues a hobby which seems very boring. Admittedly the man who loves the music of Bach may feel that others are missing something valuable and may be puzzled as to why they remain unaffected. But he is not scandalised by their failure.

---

[5]   One example. Norman Cohn writes 'Above all, it seems clear that the man who inspired the great massacres of Jews in the cities along the Rhine, Emico or Emerich, imposed himself on his followers as the Emperor of the Last Days. He was a feudal baron notorious for his ferocity but claimed to have been led to take the cross by visions and revelations sent by God'. Norman Cohn, *Pursuit of the Millennium* (Paladin, 1970), p. 73. See also John Kekes, *The Morality of Pluralism*.

[6]   Isaiah Berlin, 'The Pursuit of the Ideal' in *The Proper Study of Mankind* (Chatto and Windus, 1997), p. 7.

The way I have described these different pursuits makes them seem a paradigm of differences of values. Surely the fact that I take pleasure in doing crosswords shows that I value the activity and, by extension, the crosswords. That I do not value horse-racing is shown by the fact that I do not pore over form books or read the Sporting Times. But things are not that simple. I do think that solving crossword puzzles is a trivial pursuit. In one way I value it and in another I do not. I value it in that I look forward to opening the newspaper and hope that there will be one set by Araucaria. But a way in which I don't value it is suggested by the fact that I would regard any frustration at not having one to hand as reflecting badly on myself. Equally I do not avidly recommend doing crosswords to others. But my interest in literature or music I value in both ways. I enjoy and look forward to a concert, or to a chance to play a new piece of music or read a new book and think that those who don't share my interests are missing some of the great things in life. But I won't make very strenuous efforts to convert others, especially if their lives contain a passion for another art, such as dance, in which my interest is rather superficial. Nor am I over-worried by differences of taste or opinion.

I have spoken of 'valuing'. Harry G. Frankfurt, who has written most perceptively about these issues, speaks of 'what we care about'.[7] 'Caring' is indeed closer to ordinary talk and therefore to be preferred; it does not preclude those nuances of everyday speech which are so important in moral philosophy and which disappear when we resort to neologisms or stipulative definition. But we do well to recognise that we may care about things which we wish we did not care about. Furthermore, it is certainly not the case that caring about something makes it important to one. Do I care about finishing the crossword. I suppose so. I want to. Is it important to me? No.

Parenthetically, I have found that those who love the music of Wagner *are* annoyed when other music lovers attack the music. Indeed their reactions are interestingly

[7]   *The Importance of What We Care About* (Cambridge University Press, 1988).

similar to those of one sect of religious believers when an adjacent sect excoriates them as not true believers. A few rather absurdly offensive remarks that I made in print about Wagner drew an hysterically abusive letter from a Wagnerite a few years ago, in particular when I made the evidently true observation that an anti-Semitic interpretation of the Ring cannot be ruled out. But, in the same way, within the circle of those who breed pedigree dogs, for instance, there may be very heated differences of opinion about what sort of conformation is right. It has been suggested to me that this is because they see their own importance as depending on such matters and there is, after all, a matter of evaluation involved here. There are dog shows. The owners want their dogs to win. If the judges favour another dog, they may feel that their judgement has been slighted or worse, that the merits of their own beloved pooch have been overlooked, much as a parent might feel hurt if his child is judged to have failed an examination. For breeders, too, there may be financial considerations. Perhaps my correspondent's love for Wagner's music made it difficult to recognise what is certainly true, that Wagner was a vile man and a proto-Nazi. And that reflected on his judgement.

Yet, on the whole, those who pursue interests and who have hobbies don't seem to care that others do not share them and, quite often, they are unconcerned at differing sub-interests within their group. One enthusiast collects first editions of Waugh and another of Lawrence and they do not persecute each other. Somebody who is fanatical about the merits of first editions of Lawrence is, at worst, a bore. Even breeders of Bearded Collies don't pick quarrels with the breeders of Afghan hounds.

The problem is that the demands of religion seem, for believers, to trump all other considerations. Mere hobbies fall short of the persistent, peremptory and uncompromising claims of religion. Not to believe is thought wicked and dangerous whereas a failure to love even the music of Bach is considered neither. The late Pope viewed everybody who did not share his views on matters of religion and morality as seriously mistaken and at risk of a harsh judgement in the world to come. So it was important that he make converts to the true faith; these attitudes are to be found in other religions. Roughly, the more fervent a believer the less tolerant he is of divergent opinions. Within the believer's own religious community, such a passion is not judged as boring (though he may be quietly avoided by his co-religionists); rather he may be, officially, saintly. Somebody who talks about Jesus all the time has, like Mary, chosen the better part and the churchgoer who mutters that he is boring had better not say it too loud; the rest of the congregation is unlikely to admit that he is right. Fanaticism is not a criticism believers make of others within their fold (or, if they do make it, they show that their own involvement is not whole-hearted and therefore an occasion of offence to God).

So why is there this gap between hobbies and religions? Why cannot religion just be a hobby of a few people who leave others alone? Well, the answers are not very difficult to find. Religion has an ontology and, more relevantly, it has a morality and it is these aspects held in common with other belief systems which have led people to describe ideologies like Fascism or Communism as 'faiths'. This is what prevents religion from being a relatively harmless hobby. But as far as the ontology is concerned, there are familiar difficulties; consequently, religious commitment in the west is deeply puzzling. After the objections of Hume and other critics of religious metaphysics one would think that it should be quietly put to rest with other ancient belief systems. It seems to me very difficult for an intelligent, thoughtful and educated modern man to believe in survival after death and without that belief the threat of punishment disappears; so where, now, is the danger in unbelief? In any case the notion of an after-life is not an option which offers much to those who have lived well in this. I care far more that people should live after me and relish the seasons, the landscape, the sight of wild birds and animals, the music of Mahler and Elgar, the plays of Shakespeare and all that has made my life worth living to me. Of course, the world will not go on indefinitely but a time scale of billions means little. More significant is the fact that English will eventually move so far from Shakespeare's that the sense of his sonnets will be lost to the casual reader and not easily recovered. Worse, perhaps, is the fact that we may destroy our environment; our generation may be the first to see that the world may be, if not destroyed, rendered uninhabitable by Homo sapiens through our own activities, our greed and short-sightedness.

Many find it equally difficult to believe that a Deity exists. The factual claims made by religion, that Christ died and rose again or that he performed miracles are rejected by many who call themselves Christians. Subtract its literary distinction and what is left of the Bible; just another collection of old writings. What then is left of the content of this religion? It now ought to have no more command over us than a relatively harmless eccentricity like astrology. Yet once again, those who believe in astrology may, like the students of ouija boards or tarot cards, be rather silly but they are not a threat to their fellow human beings.

Of course, for many who have lost their faith, Christian morality remains. Indeed I suspect that, for the first generation or two of those who rejected Christianity, the idea that the Christian religion was not a repository of moral teaching of the highest order would have seemed as shocking as their own apostasy seemed to conventional Victorians. Further, I still believe that, for many, Christian morality remains something which they cling to despite their scepticism about its other claims. I am myself shocked when somebody asks 'What's wrong with selfishness?' and I do not believe that many people have been able to regard Nietzsche's objection to compassion as other than the rather distasteful showing off of a precocious and immature individual. You cannot think that a life without compassion is a better life to lead without glorying in your own nastiness. R.B. Braithwaite, in a famous lecture given half a century ago, effectively reduced religion to morality;[8] religious statements are *au fond* moral assertions which both express an attitude and convey the intention to act in a certain way,

---

[8]   R.B. Braithwaite, *An Empiricist's View of the Nature of Religious Belief* (Cambridge University Press, 1955).

consonant with a way of life. Their primary use is to announce allegiance to a set of moral principles. The stories which characterise Christian tradition, the stories in the Bible, accompany this.[9] It is a view echoed by Don Cupitt when he describes God as 'the sum of our values'.[10]

In the previous book I mentioned, I argued that, contrary to the assumptions of what I shall call minimalist or reductionist Christians (those who think that Christian morality is all that can and should be salvaged from the wreckage caused by the Higher Criticism), morality is not unaffected by its theological context. I argued that in many ways morality is damaged by being placed in such a context. I argued that it was damaged thereby because such concepts as love and trust were distorted when directed towards God and, further, that a religious context offered us 'one thought too many', as Bernard Williams would have put it. Remove God from the equation and you remove a distorting factor leaving a sounder motivation. As I say, what are virtues when displayed amongst ourselves are changed when directed at God, so that they are either no longer virtues or if they *are* it is in a much etiolated form.[11] Trust, for example, comes in various forms; it is something which may develop as we get to know somebody; we may find him to be reliable in certain matters and trust him. On the other hand, a small child, with very little experience of the world, may be said to trust its father. Or you may trust a stranger not because there is no alternative but because you value trust even where you think it may turn out to your disadvantage and you are set upon nurturing it in yourself. So in which of these cases is trust a virtue? Only, I would have thought, where you show this preparedness to trust others where it might turn out to your disadvantage. You see somebody apparently injured. You drive her to the hospital. Now in some countries, people feign injury in order to rob the Good Samaritan who gives a lift. Trust in

---

[9] For some observations see R.M. Hare, *Essays on Religion and Education*, pp. 13, 18, 23, 28.
[10] Don Cupitt, *The Sea of Faith* (SCM, 1994), p. 275.
[11] *The Moral Case against Religious Belief* (SCM, 1997).

such circumstances involves a risk and to take such a risk is virtuous. Indeed the virtuous person might not see a risk here; a virtuous innocent might simply be astonished when she is taken for a ride. But I think we rate more highly the person who is worldly wise enough to see the risk and accept it.

Now there are contexts where trust is not only central but so crucial to the relationship that no risk is to be thought of. If you love your partner or your father you do not think you take a risk in trusting. If there was any calculation of risks then the relationship would change. To anticipate somewhat, it is true that if the relationship is disturbed by one partner betraying that trust then forgiveness of the breach may change the relationship again — if not always to its original form, at least to something near it. As we shall see, forgiveness does presume a network of relationships between offender and offended for it to be intelligible though the network may be fairly exiguous. And this has implications. For precisely this reason, it might seem marginal to the concept of forgiveness to suppose that we could forgive a terrorist who has killed someone we love for the terrorist has no pre-existing relationship either with the victim or with us. The victim might complain 'But what have I done to you?' and that reveals the absence of a relationship. Now you might argue that a relationship of sorts is created by the injury. A woman is assaulted by a drunk she has never met before. She can forgive him because, like it or not, she is now involved with him in some way or other.

Be all this as it may, according to Christians, we take no risks in trusting God 'with whom there is no variableness neither shadow of turning' (James 1.17). What makes trust a virtue is absent here. The theological context, I argued, denatures virtues like love and trust, turning them into pallid versions of what is found on earth. In that earlier book my approach was rather the converse of the traditional difficulties faced by religion. Rather than the problem of what we can mean by, for example, fatherly love, when it is transposed from a human setting to apply to God, I was concerned about how the exercise of characteristically human virtues can be intelligible when aimed at a Being so remote from ourselves as a Deity. It is not the ways of describing God, metaphorical, analogical or what, which perturb. It is the problem of describing *us*.

What I took to be the great significance of these arguments was the attack on a half-way house which permits a laid-back, Laodicean attitude to dogma whilst preserving something of the content of Christianity. The advocates of this position rationalized their practices. They might have retained a few fragments of the old faith, even a belief in God, without a belief in miracles, an after-life or a resurrection. But essentially it was the product of a desire to reassemble something out of the potsherds that remained which persuaded them—with a soupcon of self-deception—that they still were Christians. I certainly spent some years in that limbo. So what function could such a theology play in morality? If it is removed then reductionist Christians have no religion left. If it remains, it distorts. So the importance of my original argument was not just that it spoke against those who maintain that religion is necessary to guarantee morality; that cannot be if morality is diluted thereby, or, more precisely, if the backing of religion is bought at a cost and the cost is too great. For the cost is the distortion of morality. It was also an argument against reductionist or minimalist accounts of religious belief showing that the residue was not what it seemed. It was not something we could value.

Our moral concepts are not always acquired in a theological context. Their acquisition is mostly too early for that to be the case and for many the religious context is too tangential to everyday living to play much of a role. Most religious people are conventionally devout. Religion does not play a huge part in their everyday lives and their moral life is not continuously under its gaze. I regard this as a thoroughly good thing. The conventionality of their religious commitment means that it does not then follow necessarily that, given a religious context, their moral ideas will be distorted. That will depend both upon the religion and on how fervent the belief of the individual is. My suspicion is that the more intense the religious devotion the more the morality is in danger. Circumspice.

There is a criticism of my attack on religion which began to surface as soon as I began to publish these ideas. It is that a sternly moralistic conception of religion allows no room for spirituality and spirituality, certainly as much as morality, is the essence of religion. The metaphysics of religion is more or less dispensable; there is a long tradition of mystical thought and experience which is independent of it. The problem I have is that I do not really understand what 'spirituality' is—other than an interest in and a concern with practising religion. It is obviously of significance in Don Cupitt's work. But without a clear understanding of what a spiritual experience is of, an understanding of the object of such an experience, it offers only an explanation obscurum per obscuris.

It is time to turn to the main topic of this book; the importance of forgiveness is undeniable. It is central to the Christian religion and I imagine it plays an important role in other religions as well. To be forgiving is virtuous[12] though forgiveness is not listed amongst the three theological virtues. Now forgiveness is a slippery concept. I shall argue that it appears in several forms and it rather depends upon which variety we have in mind whether, for example, there are any unforgivable sins or not. But part of my problem with forgiveness is rather the reverse of my problems with trusting God; it is in fact the familiar and time-honoured problem of making sense of descriptions of God. Can God forgive and if He forgives, in what sense does He forgive? For I am not here concerned with our forgiving God. Only for the rather blasphemous Omar Khayyam is forgiveness of God conceivable.

('For all the Sin wherewith the Face of Man is blackened, Man's Forgiveness give—and take!' *Rubaiyat* LVIII.)

For the orthodox believer it will not arise because God cannot harm him. My problem here is a cousin to the traditional ones. I suspect that most of us, if asked, would say

---

[12]   See Robert C. Roberts, 'Forgivingness', *American Phil. Qtly*, 32 (1995), pp. 289–306.

that being forgiving is the same sort of virtue in God as it is in human beings. I shall suggest that this cannot be the case. If God forgives He cannot forgive as human beings forgive and what is a virtue in a human being cannot be a virtue of the same sort in a Deity. This parallels some of the traditional difficulties about ascriptions to God. We may ask how God could *act, see, be a father,* etc. I am asking how He could *forgive.* I shall suggest that forgiveness in God is more akin to the exercise of mercy in judgement than it is to forgiveness in the human context. But in order to argue this, I need to inquire into what human forgiveness is and, as a beginning, I shall consider some examples. One upshot of considering these might be to show that forgiveness is 'systematically ambiguous'—as they used to say in my youth—though I find it difficult to decide whether one is dealing with two or more sufficiently different concepts of forgiveness for us to suppose the term is ambiguous or whether we should conclude that the concept is a vague one with a multiplicity of conditions. I do not know on what basis one can decide between these alternatives though many writers concur that there are various sorts of forgiveness.[13]

III

This is not a book on ethics but I need to say something about how I see the moral life. So to end this introduction, I shall sketch, briefly, the account of morality which I favour. It allows a fairly small role for obligation and duty. Obligation and duty enter where responses and imagination fail. They are a substitute for the operation of what Wittgenstein called 'primitive responses' which, I suggest, operate in tandem with the use of imagination. What I suggest is that we have Humean dispositions or Wittgensteinian 'primitive reactions' to help others in straits. John Stuart Mill's account of moral development bears similarities to this. (We have less attractive inclinations as well—to kick the dog which

---

[13] See for example Jean Harvey. 'Forgiving as an obligation of the moral life', *Int. Jnl Moral and Social Studies*, 8 (1993), pp. 211–22.

behaves in a cowed way.) The Good Samaritan was moved by the spectacle of the man who fell among thieves and helped him. But such a reaction is a reaction to what is immediately before you. You help a child who has fallen over or who is terrified and lost because you are affected by his or her plight. Even an animal may be moved to comfort the ill or upset. But what about children in distant towns or other countries; we do not see them and consequently do not react as we do to what is before us — or what about those who will come after us and for whom we may feel we should have a concern that the earth remain to provide sustenance in a climate that is not hostile? We have imaginative powers that animals and small children lack. We can imagine how we would react; we imagine we are present to see their plight and we act accordingly; in the same way, I might, while driving too fast, imagine a child running into the road, imagine that I could not brake in time, imagine the grief of the parents and this will make me slow down. (As I have observed already, I am not denying that there are primitive responses to hurt something, nor denying that the imagination may, in evil people, be used to think up tortures. This is all true.) For me duty is a second-best; the ethics I propose is rooted in the particular and it is imagination which enables us to move beyond this. Duty or obligation are poor substitutes for a richer moral life, a product of reactions and the play of the imagination.[14] So what I argue is that we should think of duty as a substitute for the role of the imagination, a substitute which operates when our imaginative faculty is deficient or where we have not time to reflect. It is imagination which should provide the generalising tendency. The Kantian, Utilitarian or Hare-style emphasis on universalisability or universalisation is replaced, on this scheme, with the operation of the imagination. It is imagination which enables us to act prudently with respect to our future needs and concern ourselves with the fortunes of others. Any Kantian style ethics which

[14] For an alternative see Christine M. Korsgaard, *The Sources of Normativity* (Cambridge University Press, 1996). My views appear at greater length in 'Moral Tales', *Philosophy* (1992).

places a primary emphasis on duty chooses the lesser. Later on we shall see what role this has in the case of forgiveness.

Because I can imagine, or even visualise, what it was like for the victims of the Asian Tsunami to lose their children, to see them borne away on waves and be unable to reach them, my imagination enables me to be moved by their plight. It is more vivid if they are before me, of course, but stories which train the imagination can develop the capacity to react to distant tragedies. I assume that politicians who wage war set aside such matters; they choose not to imagine the consequences. Perhaps some of them have perverse passions; the thought of cruelty excites them and they fantasise about it; for some of them the idea of having within their power people whom they can torture is deeply satisfying. Or they may be mistaken about matters of fact. I suppose if you really believed that Jews were a threat to health you might feel that you had the unpleasant duty of eradicating them. You might believe it right to burn heretics or extirpate unbelievers. Some philosophers take the view that such perverse moral principles are only possible to the extent they derive from errors of fact.[15] Thus the truly moral Nazi would not be proceeding directly from a perverse moral principle such as 'Cruelty is a good thing and should be encouraged wherever possible'. Rather he imagined a world without Jews, homosexuals, gypsies, Slavs, the mentally deranged and the physically deformed as a world of light and innocence, an Edenic scene in which blond giants frolicked amongst the forests and streams, rejoicing in *bruderschaft* and *gemeinschaft*. He did not enjoy the cruelty involved in bringing this about; it was a necessary precondition; he who wills the ends must will the means. A less moral Nazi might act on the moral law — perverted only in the sense that it derives from crazy errors of fact. He is not motivated by the thought of a paradise on earth but by obedience to the law; many Nazis would have been in this category. Which leaves us with those who enjoyed cruelty — those few people to be found in any society who have not been inhibited by social

[15]   See Ronald Milo, *Immorality*, p. 51.

development from indulging their liking for hurting and humiliating others.

I spoke of 'primitive responses'. Indeed I think that it is the existence of such responses to hurt and suffering which underlies the moral life. (So far, so Humean.) Am I some sort of moral realist? I am rather anxious to avoid general discussions of ethics and morality in this book. This is partly because the literature is enormous and sophisticated. It is also because I think that moral considerations are both so various and so variegated as to make a general account of morality unlikely. Yes, utilitarian considerations operate sometimes in making moral decisions; yes sometimes, a Kantian universalisability criterion seems relevant. Morality is as complicated as human beings are (very) and it is unlikely that a general theory will be found satisfactory. There will always be aspects of our moral life, our decisions, our judgements and our dilemmas which it fails to catch. Partly this is because moral dilemmas seem of the essence of the moral life.

Chapter Two

To Forgive is Human, to Judge Divine

> Further he commanded us all to forgive these people, but never to trust them, for they had been most false to him and to those that gave them power, and he feared also to their souls.[1]

I: Christian Forgiveness

It was a few years ago that a couple of news reports set me thinking about the nature of forgiveness. They stuck in my mind as initially puzzling but the puzzlement was at first rather undefined — philosophers know how it is with philosophy. My teacher, Stefan Korner, used to speak of his 'philosophical stomach'; it gave him an inkling that something was wrong but he did not know what. (It is a sort of Socratic demon or a converse of the Quaker's 'inner light' — 'inner darkness' in this case.) Both examples are cases where a Christian minister forgave those who injured his daughter. In the first case, burglars broke into a West London vicarage and one of them raped the daughter of the Vicar; in the second a Methodist minister lost his daughter in the Enniskillen Remembrance Day bombings. One oddity in the first case was that the Vicar forgave even though he, although injured, as any father would be, was not the prime sufferer. It was his daughter who was raped. I imagine the press could not get at her and so asked the father the

---

[1] The Princess Elizabeth, the 13-year-old daughter of Charles I, from her memoir of her last meeting with her father the day before his execution, written the night before his death.

fatuous question which seems always on the lips of journal-
ists nowadays—'but how do you feel?' He replied in the
way he was expected to reply. Now we will surely think
that, in this instance it was for the daughter to forgive, if that
were possible and proper. The immediacy of her father's
response could not but seem to trivialise a grotesque and
shattering offence. (I have been told that the daughter did
not forgive her assailant.)[2]

What makes the Vicar's response more puzzling still is
that it is usually harder to forgive those who offend those
you love than it is to forgive those who offend you. Senator
Wilson, whose daughter was killed by the IRA, was in the
prime position to forgive because his daughter, who I take it
was injured by this, was dead. But the Vicar's daughter was
still alive. 'I shall try to forgive him' might have been a more
timely response, perhaps. (Parenthetically there might be a
Christian answer to this difficulty, possibly an answer
which might be shared with Islam and Judaism. It would be
that what turns an act into a process is God's grace, which
makes possible the change of heart which a form of words
alone does not bring. God will change me so that I genuinely
forgive. However this is not an option open to an atheist
like myself. We have no place for 'grace' in our repertoire of
concepts.)

So apart from the problem that the wrong person seemed
to be offering the forgiveness, what puzzled me about the
Vicar's reply was the rapidity of the response, something it
shared with my second example. Now of course, you can
explain that by reference to the man's position as a Christian
minister. Like God, *c'est son metier*. But why should it be so
puzzling? Why should we think that more time would be
seemly? (Perhaps I should say here that what happened to
this girl and to the two ministers is so dreadful that one
must feel a bit uncomfortable about using it to introduce a
philosophical problem. But trivial cases really won't help
here and I prefer to use actual examples where possible.)
The philosophically significant concern draws on just this,

---

[2]   Trudy Govier. *Forgiveness and Revenge* (Routledge, 2002), pp. 65–8,
       has another excellent example of what I discuss here.

the promptness of the forgiveness, and my starting point here reflects a concern which has been at the very fountain-head of recent discussion of forgiveness, since the nineteen seventies. Can forgiveness be merely what I earlier and perhaps unfairly called a 'form of words' and what the philosopher J.L. Austin called a 'speech act'? (If I say 'I promise to see you at 11.00 tomorrow' I act through what I say. My speech act binds me. By these words I do something. I act. In his earlier work on speech acts, Austin called this a 'performative utterance.') It seems fairly obvious that forgiveness cannot be a speech act for the following reason. If I promise to do x and do not do it, you will not say 'Obviously, you did not promise after all' but if I say 'I forgive you' but then show animosity and resentment when the matter comes up again, you are entitled to say 'You said you forgave me but obviously you did not'. That we can say of some offence 'it is hard to forgive' suggests as well that forgiveness is not a speech act but rather that a process is involved which can be hard to accomplish.[3] And yet religious people often speak as though it is just a speech act and some philosophers defend this. Whether this is encouraged by the Lord's Prayer where it seems that forgiveness is treated as an action, I am not certain. It might be that Jesus thought of forgiveness as an act but I don't imagine that we can be sure. Even if we treat 'I forgive you' as a performative which states a refusal to prosecute or seek revenge, as has been suggested by some who think it can be a speech act, it does not seem on all fours with a speech act such as promising.[4] If you forgave and then sought revenge, the offender would be entitled to say not 'But you forgave me', thus paralleling 'You promised me' but 'You *said* you forgave me' (but you did not). In which case, there seems no logical difficulty with forgiving being subsequently withdrawn or with the offended thinking she has forgiven when she has not. Indeed, in so much as forgiveness *can* be an act it seems to

---

[3]   See R.S. Downie, 'Forgiveness', *Philosophical Quarterly* 15 (1965), pp. 128–34.

[4]   See W.R. Neblett, 'Forgiveness and Ideals', *Mind* 83 (1974), pp. 269–75.

collapse into the notion of pardoning. These reflections endorse the assumption, quite widespread, that forgiveness is multi-faceted.[5]

In my two anecdotes it seems that forgiveness is being offered as though it were something you could do straight off and there is much in the Christian and Jewish tradition which encourages this. It might be argued that one aspect of forgiveness is that the offence is no longer counted as part of the offender's moral history, so to speak. Jean Harvey[6] speaks of not calculating the offence in the offender's present moral status and this enables us to think of forgiveness as both an act and consequently as an obligation. But there are problems in making this idea sufficiently precise; it is hard to see what this 'calculation' amounts to. After all, I do not forget that the offence has occurred. The suspicion remains that not much has been added in such a way as to 'explain' the notion of forgiveness to us.

So forgiveness is supposed to involve a change of heart and attitude in the forgiver. This seems to be the notion of forgiveness central to Christian thought. I said that what is puzzling about both my examples is that insufficient time seems to have elapsed for this to take place. As I said, Christianity does, sometimes, seem to treat forgiveness as an act of will which may be made voluntarily and if this is so then 'I forgive' ought indeed to be just a speech act. It seems then to be very like a judicial act of pardon. In the Old Testament we find a list of offences which can be forgiven providing a sacrifice is made. Sinning in ignorance is dealt with by the sacrifice of an unblemished female goat. 'The Priest shall make an atonement for him and it shall be forgiven him' (Lev. 4.31). The sin is expunged through the appropriate ritual. Once forgiven it would make no sense to call for further reparations. This quasi-legal notion does not seem to be very close to our modern conception of forgiveness though, as I suggest, it may provide the root for a treatment which

---

[5]   See Geoffrey Scarre, *After Evil; Responding to Wrongdoing* (Ashgate, Aldershot, 2004). Scarre describes evil as multi-faceted but gives reasons to draw the same conclusion about forgiveness.

[6]   *op. cit.*, p. 215.

turns forgiveness into a speech act. For us, forgiveness is not conditional on reparation being made in the way that we find in the Old Testament and that suggests that the word translated as 'forgive' is rather remote from our current conception. In fact, if reparation is made to the offended person then forgiveness is no longer an issue; it is redundant. And if I forgive, then subsequent reparation is embarrassing; it revives what we are trying to put aside.

Now the matter of reparation relates to another issue central to any discussion of forgiveness and that is repentance. If the offender voluntarily makes reparation then he acknowledges that he is at fault. I have spoken of a change of heart in the offended. What about a change of heart in the offender? Christian writers on forgiveness generally make repentance a requirement for forgiveness. This is also the main Jewish tradition. It can be described in these words. Forgiveness is primarily viewed as God's forgiveness of man, a forgiveness which results in reconciliation with Him. A major tradition in Christian thought is the idea that Christ's sacrifice justifies us in the sight of God in as much as He sets matters right and restores our relationship with Him. A classic book in the evangelical tradition, H.R. Mackintosh's 'The Christian Experience of Forgiveness', treats forgiveness as a specifically theological concept. Mackintosh is almost entirely concerned with God's forgiveness of man and the human experience of forgiving one another plays a very small role and a role which is evidently parasitic on the theological. We need to be forgiven because, primarily, we have disobeyed God, for God has a right to the obedience which it is in our nature to give. (I shall have more to say about 'obedience' later in this chapter.) On this conception forgiveness is a theological notion with judicial elements. Belief in Christ allows us to have conferred upon us a valid righteousness.[7] Of course, many theologians have queried how this may be so and their criticisms are telling.[8]

---

[7]   H.R. Mackintosh, The *Christian Experience of Forgiveness* (1927), p. 112.

[8]   In *God and the Bible* (1875) (pp. 18–19), Matthew Arnold describes the doctrine of justification by atonement in terms of 'a sort of infinitely

It is hard to see how somebody else's suffering the penalty
for my sin can be either fair or serve justice. It is I who
offended, after all. It is simply unfair for somebody else to
be punished in my stead. Now somebody might pay a fine
on my behalf of course, and my debt be settled thereby. But
my guilt remains despite all this. Some seem to think that
God can only forgive us because His son has suffered on the
cross so as to make restitution for our offences; this is certainly a major element in Christian accounts of forgiveness.
But this muddles up matters of justice and matters of moral
guilt. Not only is it hard to see how the guilt of my offence
could be cancelled by somebody else repaying it on my
behalf and harder still to understand how a single death
could do this for billions or the thousands whose crimes are
vastly greater than any I have committed, but to suppose
that God needs his son to die before He can forgive us exag-
gerates the crimes of most of us and places God Himself in a
poor light. Furthermore, the offences remain and they cannot be wiped out. Nor can it be the case that forgiveness
becomes possible only when the sentence has been served,
whether vicariously or not. If it does become possible that
would be no more than a psychological oddity of the
forgiver. The relatives of somebody cruelly done to death
might feel that nothing could count as 'paying the price' or
'serving one's time' and the exaction of the penalty is

---

magnified and improved Lord Shaftesbury, with a race of vile
offenders to deal with, whom his natural goodness would incline
him to let off, only his sense of justice will not allow it; then a younger
Lord Shaftesbury, on the scale of his father and very dear to him, who
might live in grandeur and splendour if he liked, but who prefers to
leave his home, to go and live among the race of offenders, and to be
put to an ignominious death, on condition that his merits shall be
counted against their demerits, and that his father's goodness shall
be restrained no longer from taking effect, but any offender shall be
admitted to the benefit of it on simply pleading the satisfaction made
by the son—and then, finally, a third Lord Shaftesbury, still on the
same high scale, who keeps very much in the background, and works
in a very occult manner, but very efficaciously nevertheless, and who
is busy in applying everywhere the benefits of the son's satisfaction
and the father's goodness.' Braithwaite quotes it (*ibid*). The hostility
this passage aroused presumably accounts for its removal from later
editions of this book.

neither a necessary nor a sufficient condition for forgiving. If the assumption that it *is* is deeply embedded in Christian thought it is because of the quasi-legal notion of forgiveness inherited from the Jewish tradition. In 2002, the BBC showed a documentary on a former German soldier, long settled in this country and now with an English grandchild, who is tormented by the atrocities he saw and by his own part in shooting Russian prisoners of war in World War II. He cannot forget and cannot 'lighten up' as some of his friends ask him to do. Nothing can now be done about it. To suppose that God can wipe out the evil of the offence by His forgiveness is just an illusion. He may 'wipe away all tears from our eyes' but even He cannot undo the past. One remark struck me. Henry Mettelman said 'To say sorry would be ridiculous'. The crimes are of a magnitude which dwarf any attempt at apology. As well repeat Nietzsche's mantra 'what doesn't kill you makes you stronger' to a survivor from Auschwitz.

The horrendous offences committed in the last century cannot be expunged, the evil done cannot be ameliorated or wiped out by anybody, including God. These things have been done. The suffering is part of history. The view of the world as a vale of soul-making makes sense of some minor suffering. Heavy criticism of my behaviour may be painful but it may bring me to my senses. But the death of a child can hardly be justified on the grounds that it may bring the parents closer to God. To use the suffering of one as a means to benefit another would be monstrous and cannot be part of a good God's plan for the world. This case is made with immense power by Dostoevsky in 'The Karamazov Brothers' just prior to the fable of the Grand Inquisitor (Book 5, chapter 3). Ivan has described to his pious brother Alyosha how the eight-year old son of a serf hurt the paw of a favourite hound by throwing a stone. In front of the child's mother, the general who owns the serfs sets his dogs upon the child; the boy is torn to pieces.

> I want to see the lion lying down with the lamb with my own eyes, and the murdered rising up and embracing their murderers. I want to be here when everyone suddenly

finds out the why and the wherefore of everything. This is
the desire on which all religions on earth are based, and I
am a believer. But then, what about the children, what shall
I do about them? That's the question I cannot answer. For
the hundredth time I repeat — the questions are endless, but
I am only considering the children because in their case
what I have to say is incontrovertibly clear. Listen: if everybody has to suffer in order to bring about eternal harmony
through that suffering, tell me, please, what have children
to do with this? It's quite incomprehensible that they too
should have to suffer, that they too should have to pay for
harmony by their suffering. Why should they be the grist to
someone else's mill, the means of ensuring someone's
future harmony?

The question of evil is a large one. Not only is it an issue in
its own right but it is also closely related to the question of
what and who we can forgive. If there is the unforgivable it
may coincide with what is evil or may, perhaps, form a
sub-class of it.[9] This is certainly a major issue for anybody
engaging with the topic and I shall discuss it in chapter four.

Nevertheless I have come to concur with Mackintosh on
one important point; I believe that forgiveness as conceived
by the two ministers in my opening examples must be a
primarily theological and legal conception for only then can
the conflicts which lie within it be resolved.[10] However I
shall suggest that they are resolved at the price of the rich
and complex notion of forgiveness which involves a change
of heart, a conception which lies at the centre of Christian
thinking on this topic. On a thinner conception of forgiveness, it does not so much require a change of heart as the
setting aside of reparation and punishment. On this
conception, forgiveness can be a performative.

I said that Mackintosh has little to say about human forgiveness. What he does say overeggs the pudding somewhat though it seems to capture, to some extent, the

---

[9]   See also Gordon Graham, *Evil and Christian Ethics* (Cambridge
       University Press, 2001).
[10]   H.R. Mackintosh, *The Christian Experience of Forgiveness* (1927). See
       also Philip. L. Quinn, 'Christian Atonement and Kantian
       Justification', *Faith and Philosophy*, 3, 4 (1986), pp. 440–62. See as well
       Meirlys Lewis on Forgiveness, *Phil.Qtly*, 30 (1980), pp. 236–45.

psychological element involved in many Christian conceptions of forgiveness. It is necessary that we

> enter by passionate imagination and self-projection into the other's conflict, to hold by intercession his faltering hand, to weep with his sorrow, actually to think self still at other's side in the misery and loneliness of guilt — all this is requisite.

(What even if he has only borrowed my favourite album and forgotten to return it?) Mackintosh certainly has no place for one current alternative conception of forgiveness much debated by Christian thinkers, and that is unconditional forgiveness.[11] Unconditional forgiveness occurs when the injured party forgives regardless of whether the offender shows regret, remorse or makes reparation.[12] The orthodox conception of conditional forgiveness, on the other hand, requires repentance on the part of the offender. The first has been described recently by the Chief Rabbi, Jonathan Sacks, and by the Archbishop of Canterbury, Rowan Williams. It does not seem, then, to be specifically Christian. It is, perhaps, the higher virtue. (Then if you subscribe to a theodicy in which natural evils such as illness are justified because they provide scope for such virtues as compassion and forbearance, you should try to avoid remorse when you offend a bishop, priest or deacon. If I spill red wine over the Bishop at a party, he would be advised to get his forgiveness in first — to adapt the words of the famous Welsh rugby coach, Carwyn James. The Bishop, of course, needs only not to know whether or not I am remorseful for this higher form of forgiveness to take place.) In my two examples, the minister concerned 'forgave' the offender without waiting to see whether the offender expressed remorse. Indeed, in the latter case, he forgave

---

[11] The possibility of this leads Kolnai to speak of the 'paradoxy' in forgiveness. Aurel Kolnai, 'Forgiveness' in *Ethics, Value and Reality* (Athlone, 1977).

[12] Much discussed in recent literature. See Eve Garrard and David McNaughton, 'In Defence of Unconditional Forgiveness', *Proc. Aristotelian Soc.*, vol. 103 (2002), pp. 39–60 and Christopher Bennett, 'Personal and Redemptive Forgiveness', *European Journal of Philosophy*, 11 (2003), pp. 127–44.

before he knew who the offender was. Both were thus cases of 'unconditional forgiveness'. Both Jonathan Sacks and Rowan Williams make the point that it offers a means of 'breaking with the past'.[13] Rowan Williams describes it as deciding 'not to pass on the hurt but to absorb it' and Sacks as 'the action that is not reaction'. To illustrate this with what is probably at the forefront of the mind of the Chief Rabbi: at some point the Palestinians have to absorb the land seizures by the Israelis and stop suicide bombings and the Israelis to desist from further acts of repression. This may not be forgiveness; it could be an act of *realpolitik* which is what, perhaps, has happened to some extent in Ulster. But there is no doubt that forgiveness requires as a necessary condition that you pass up the chance of revenge. Perhaps a more striking example of what they describe might be marital infidelity. One partner neglects the other; she really does not care too much about his feelings or welfare. If he is ill, she seems unconcerned. He is miserable and vulnerable. A vulnerable man can attract the attention of women who think they can help him. A woman begins to talk to him; he unburdens himself; they begin an affair; he is racked with guilt. His wife finds out and, feeling herself at liberty, begins an affair with another man, already married, who will, she imagines, treat her as she ought to be treated. So another marriage is damaged. Somebody in this chain needs to absorb the hurt and stop the cycle. But, in a way, it will be at the cost of a life. The man must stay with a partner who ill-treats and despises him. He, at the same time, hurts somebody who loves him, at least pro tem.

The problem with the Christian notion of forgiveness is that it seems to meld two distinct and incompatible elements; forgiveness as an act of pardon which may be a speech act and therefore can be done straight off as a matter of obligation and forgiveness as something proceeding from the doctrine of universal love. If we love one another then we must forgive the wrongs done to us.

---

[13] A conception which may run back to Hannah Arendt, *The Human Condition* (University of Chicago, 1974), pp. 236–43.

The universal love Christianity enjoins cannot be the same sort of thing as the love you have for your wife, husband or lover or for your parents, children or friends. You cannot concern yourself with others to that extent, nor should you. You have special duties and special relationships which take priority. You can still care about the fate of people you do not know or only know briefly. Sometimes a chance acquaintance on a train or flight may strike you as a warm and approachable personality in whose company you feel comfortable. But even such transitory affection does not come up to what is required of the Christian doctrine of love. William Blake said that it is easier to forgive an enemy than a friend. If Blake is right, and I think that he is — though it rather depends on the scale of the offence — then it presumably relates to the fact that trust has been breached when a friend betrays you. Assuming then that the offence is of equal magnitude between friend and foe, the underlying thought must be something like the following. Suppose a friend cheats you at cards. (He has been a friend for some time but you have not played cards with him before.) Assume, too, that your friendship is untroubled up to this time. The offence breaches the trust between you. On the other side, you have no great expectations concerning your enemy and trust plays no central role here. The problem comes when there is an attempt to resuscitate trust. Would this be something like an act of will? Would it be like Prospero's 'I do forgive thee, unnatural as thou art'? Here warmth towards the offender, the element which makes forgiveness so hard to conceive as an action, is absent. So whilst still feeling injured (and in that sense unable to forgive) you may yet trust your friend, say by agreeing to another game, this time for money. In this sense you may forgive, if forgiveness is the right word here. You are certainly acting as if nothing has occurred and that might amount to a rather exiguous form of forgiveness. What is difficult to resuscitate is the sort of cordiality which exists between friends or between colleagues who are not particularly close, a cordiality surely required by the rich Christian notion of forgiveness. The discomfort that remains is the more acute because you have to live in the same house, or share an office with the person who has offended you. It may not be resentment; indeed it may be more like embarrassment. But it seems quite possible that you have forgiven the offender.

So what should we think of Blake's aphorism? There is this truth in it. I can act with respect to my enemy as I do with my friend. I may trust him, knowing I take a chance — but I shall not be hurt by his treachery. He cannot let me down. The fuller elements of forgiveness — relevant in the case of a friend — are necessarily absent, the elements which make it possible for me to say ' I thought you forgave me but you did not', are not there. They need not be and so the forgiveness of an enemy *is* easier than the forgiveness of a friend.

II: Renouncing Revenge

How did the Vicar in my opening example forgive? We must suppose that he was not lying. Did he really forgive the rapist or only think he did? Would we say that he only really forgave him if he had confronted the distress of his daughter and her injuries and at the same time, seen the background and history of the rapist? What if the rapist showed no remorse or even laughed at the misery of his victim. What then? Could the Vicar still be said to forgive him? Did he love him and want to meet him or was his forgiveness more like that pressed on the Princess Elizabeth in my epigraph. Perhaps the Vicar merely desired that no further harm befall the offender. How could we know that real forgiveness had taken place? Only by that?

The BBC documentary 'The Sun says sorry … and other tales of forgiveness,'[14] recounted the story of Ray and Vi Donovan whose son was murdered by three young men who 'used his head as a football'. The first reaction of Mr Donovan was to want to do the same to the murderers but, as he explained, he was a Christian and he felt he had to forgive the murderers and determined to do so. He had to

[14]   BBC 2, Feb. 14th 2005.

live the life he professed. Mrs Donovan objected strongly; she was filled with rage and hatred and would have killed them had she the chance. But when, at the trial, she saw the defendants shaking and crying and saw the effect on their families, she changed. With the verdict, she felt none of the jubilation that apparently meets a guilty verdict in the USA. There were no winners and she was glad to put the matter to rest. The Donovans wrote to one of the guilty men to say that they forgave him.

I don't know what process was involved in Mr Donovan's forgiveness; it was clearer in the case of Mrs Donovan. But he spoke as though he had decided to forgive — and this I find a little puzzling — though his conclusion, that the murderers should not feel that anybody was, on their release, out to injure or kill them might be viewed as the essence of a second form of forgiveness, the form I discuss in this section. He wishes no further harm to the criminals. (I shall explain why I have added the important rider 'further' a little later on.) This form of forgiveness is 'thinner' than the Christian sense but without doubt it is forgiveness. Certainly it is not the case that the murder no longer counts or matters; the criminals would serve their sentence and none of these lives could ever be the same again. But revenge had been set aside. This is the essence of the second form of forgiveness.

Suppose you decide, like Mr Donovan, that you will neither seek revenge nor seek redress against the offender. You could, perhaps, sue him for damages but choose not to. Have you necessarily forgiven him? I do not think so. What I have described may not always count as forgiveness — though it does in their case, partly because of the magnitude of the offence. Suppose the offence is less significant; somebody has bilked you; you cannot be bothered to pursue the matter. You want to put the whole business behind you. It then seems less like forgiveness and this would certainly be the case if you regard the perpetrator with a certain contempt. What do we make of the daughter of Charles I, mentioned in my epigraph? If she followed her father's injunction and did not trust the regicides, could she have forgiven them? What would this amount to? Would it be merely the wish that no more harm befall them than they had already done to themselves? (In fact, upon the Restoration, several of the regicides met the terrible death of being hanged, drawn and quartered.)

Another question is relevant. If it is hard to deal with and neutralise resentment, why should it not be equally hard to neutralise the wish that harm should come to your enemies? Just as resentment may nag at you, refusing to go away and constantly reappearing—to your chagrin—so perhaps might the wish that your enemy be damaged in some way. But I do not think that wishes resist our command in quite the same way. It might be that, underneath, you continue to harbour ill-will and that this shows itself in gloating when your enemy suffers a setback. This might be so but it still need not amount really to wanting his downfall and being prepared to do something about it. If you wish to get even with somebody, your wish will be operative unless it is countermanded by a wish not to—either because you think it is beneath you or because you think that retaliation is wrong or from cowardice. You might be well aware that you will get over the matter in time and these considerations may prevent you from acting on that wish. All things considered, you do not wish him ill. If a wish continues unacted on, only to reveal itself later in gloating when the offender comes to a sticky end, then what we have looks more like continued resentment than anything else. But in this case your resentment, though existing, is inert.

Now some thinkers make a case for revenge. Those philosophers who think that the vindictive passions do have a part to play in a decent life tend to stress the importance of self-respect.[15] This, together with considerations of self-defence and respect for the moral law militate against forgiveness. Failure to resent does not, they argue, show sufficient respect for the moral order which the offender has infringed. Obviously, and they will concede this, vindictiveness can be overdone. One cannot justify pursuing the

---

[15]   See Jeffrie G. Murphy, *Getting Even* (Oxford University Press, 2003).

offender at enormous cost to oneself or to the disadvantage of third parties. It may be that a cutting remark will be the appropriate response, measured and proportionate and, with that, the business is over. I might relish the opportunity to review a book by an author who, I think, reviewed me unfairly.

The problem I have with this is really threefold. Firstly keeping tabs and awaiting the opportunity to hit back looks like a petty keeping of scores. Secondly, although a riposte may be appropriate it is better if it is immediate and witty and with such replies it is hard to preserve a sense of proportion. Life would be poorer without celebrated put-downs; though perhaps most of the wittiest were either worked out in advance or are examples of *esprit d'escalier*.[16] Finally we cannot get away from the fact that 'vindictiveness' has a pejorative tone absent from 'resentment'. We do not live in an honour culture and we may be thankful for that.

I may well resent what has been done to me. I may think I have been unfairly treated and resent it. My point is rather that my resentment is not caused by the action seeming to pay me too little respect. That is not the injury. The injury is the unfairness and the consequences of the unfairness. Now reflect a little further. It would be irrational of me to allow my self-respect to be affected by another's wrong-doing. If the offender fails to pay me the respect which is my due, that is, he is insufficiently considerate of my feelings and what is due to me as a colleague or a neighbour or a family member, then it is he who has fallen in esteem. A recent member of the British Labour government had the reputation of bullying his civil servants to the point that they were terrified lest they be selected to read to him the Sunday papers. He failed to treat them decently but *their* status was not reduced by his displays of childish temper at hostile coverage. His was. My reaction to somebody injuring me ought to be sadness at the fact that she has injured me. I do not deny, of course, that

---

[16] As when Margot Asquith corrected Jean Harlow's mispronunciation of her name (she pronounced the 't' at the end of Margot): ' The "t" is silent, as in "Harlow".'

one's self-respect may be damaged by somebody else's insult but the remedy is not revenge. It lies in educating yourself not to take such insults as reflecting the way things really are. Admittedly an insult might bring to my attention features of myself with which I am rather unhappy but then the experience may be salutary and forgiveness is not relevant.

The integrity and goodness of the Donovans was remarkable and those who advocate vindictiveness ought to see this moving documentary. The Donovan's sense of self-respect required them to forgive and their sense of what the moral law requires equally demanded that they forgive. Regardless of whether an appeal to the moral law plays any role in our moral lives, the attempt to buttress vindictiveness by an appeal to these considerations is simply question-begging. The self-respect of a vindictive man may require vindictiveness but that is because he prizes it. The Donovans did not. They would not respect themselves if they did not forgive.

Curiously the idea that the bad man or woman injures herself in what he or she does seems to play little part in recent writing on forgiveness and in the discussions of punishment which often accompany it. A selfish person is somebody most of us would avoid. It is natural to think of this in terms of consequences. The selfish man is bound to lose out. Yet if a selfish life is a bad life to live, and many of us would agree upon that, it may not be that this is to be understood just in terms of the damage done to other people or, indeed, to the environment. The selfish man may injure himself. But I would prefer to think that the damage is not just in terms of the consequences for himself. It can be more direct. Socrates thought that the evil-doer is to be pitied. He thought it worse to do evil than to suffer evil.[17] The evil-doer may look out on a world in which everybody is out for himself. His own grudging and self-interested cooperation will make him unwilling to recognise disinterested generosity in others. He will mistakenly think of them as dupes or

---

[17] The classical discussion is, of course, in Plato's *Gorgias* 468ff. See also St.Augustine, *Confessions*, trans. Pine-Coffin (Penguin, 1961), p. 39.

fools. So the nastiness he shows comes out in a distorted view of the world; in the same way a career politician probably does not take at face value what is sincerely stated but looks for an intent to benefit the speaker or his party. The consequence of a Socratic view is that punishment, as opposed to protecting society from the offender, ceases to play a role. The offender has already injured himself and he has injured himself in proportion to the magnitude of his crime; we are no longer presented with the problem of making the punishment fit the crime; that is catered for already in his self-harm. Protecting society then becomes the issue as far as 'punishment' is concerned. Ray Gaita imagines the criminal saying to himself in horror 'What have I done?' We often say of some crime, 'I would not want to have that on my conscience' and that well expresses the idea that you simply do not want to be such a man or such a woman. It is important to note that on this conception the evil-doer has injured himself whether or not he recognises it. He may think it fine to be a drug-pusher or to be so violent that others 'fear' him. (His self-deception will lead him to describe this as 'respect'.) But others see that this is not so.

This is not to deny that there are many other ways in which your life may be damaged, such as through an untimely bereavement. You may also be damaged, possibly irrevocably, by an accident in which you were an agent, though not yourself responsible. A train driver once told me of a colleague who, rounding a bend at speed, saw a tiny girl sitting on the line. He had no chance to pull up. He was unable to drive again.

If we allow an exiguous form of forgiveness which means abandoning the wish for revenge, then there need be no unforgivable sins; on the contrary the richer conception of Christian forgiveness is compatible with there being offences too grave for the offended to forgive in that sense without minimising the offences. But we may still wish the perpetrators no further harm than the harm they have already done to themselves. The crimes of the holocaust seem to me to be in that category but that is an issue I turn to in a later chapter.

III: Benign Neglect or 'Letting Go'

A fourth example leads me to the surrogate for forgiveness which it is a main purpose of this chapter to propose. In Zhang Ymou's very fine film *To Live* (1994), the protagonist Fugai loses his only son in an accident; an old comrade from the years of the revolution, Chunsheng, runs his car into a wall which crushes the child. At the funeral Chunsheng offers a wreath and money, only to be driven away with abuse. He leaves, saying, 'I owe you a life'. They meet from time to time but Jiazhen, Fugai's wife, refuses to speak to Chunsheng. Late one night he visits them. Fugai steps outside to speak. Chunsheng has been denounced by the Party and is ruined; worse, his wife has committed suicide. 'Take the money', he says. Jiazhen overhears and invites Chunsheng in, her first act of reconciliation. He refuses and as he walks away, she calls after him 'Remember, you still owe us a life; you must value yours'.

I do not know whether this amounts to forgiveness because I don't know whether Chinese culture has a concept which is equivalent to ours at all points. The attempt at reconciliation comes only after Chunsheng has lost somebody. There is an approximate balance. (Is there, behind this, an assumption that in this world fortune constitutes a fixed stock and that somebody else's good fortune means that it is less likely you will receive some? Chunsheng's ill fortune cancels out his earlier success.) Does this attempt at reconciliation amount to forgiveness? It may not quite be that. Nevertheless, there are some connections here. Time has passed and that surely makes a difference; it might lead us to think that this might approximate to forgiveness; there is the sense that Chunsheng and Jiazhen could now talk about the past. This, as I shall suggest, is significant. If they chose not to it would be for fear of a misunderstanding or from a fear of embarrassment but not because of a fear of opening old wounds. If forgiveness is at issue, then, if resentment were to flare up again, it would be fair for the other party to declare 'You said you forgave but you obviously did not'.

Robert C. Roberts[18] speaks of the way the suffering of the person who has offended you 'casts into the shadow' grounds for anger. It is an illuminating turn of phrase but, as he is aware, uncertainty remains as to whether we should construe this as being some sort of causal condition for forgiveness or whether it is part of forgiving itself. Does it bring forgiveness about or is it something inherent in it? He draws an example from *War and Peace*. In the military hospital after the Battle of Borodino, Prince Andrei meets the rake who attempted to seduce his fiancee; the rake has had his leg amputated. Does Andrei's compassion amount to forgiveness? Our uncertainty here reflects the slipperiness of the concept of forgiveness.

Whatever the facts of the matter here, what is interesting in both examples is that time has passed. In contrast with the idea of forgiveness as being an act, I want to draw attention to something which may not be forgiveness as usually conceived but which might be mistaken for it. What I want to propose is an alternative to forgiveness as Christians describe it. I think it is a reaction to injury which is more common though we seem to have no commonly used word for it. I am going to describe it as 'benign neglect'. 'Neglect' is offered by Webster as a part synonym for forgiveness. Chambers offers as an alternative, 'disregard'. The 1971 Oxford English Dictionary has 'to cease to harbour' and 'pardon'. 'To cease to harbour' comes very close to what I suggest is involved but I do not think it can be taken as a direct equivalent or definition of 'forgive' which is what is suggested by the OED. 'Pardon', of course, is open to the problem that it implies an *act* of pardoning as opposed to 'benign neglect' and thus displays the very problems we found in the notion of forgiveness conceived purely as something we can do. What I am going to describe is not an

---

[18] Robert C. Roberts, 'Forgivingness', *American Phil. Qtly*, 32 (1995), pp. 289–306, see p. 297.

action and it may not be something which is attempted, intended or pursued; it does not carry so much baggage as the Christian notion. It can just happen.[19]

So the alternative to an *act* of forgiveness will be something like this. A friend says something cutting and unfair to you. You feel injured and resentful. But the weeks go by; neither of you mentions the matter to the other and relations return to their former equable ways. The sense of injury fades. An apology from the offender might have helped the process along but none was forthcoming. You have not forgotten but the injury no longer matters. At no point have you 'decided to forgive'; there was no 'act of forgiveness'. Indeed if you were now to make explicit the forgiveness you would be making a song and dance about it which might well damage the rapprochement. You have decided that it would be petty to persist. 'Life is too short', or 'Let bygones be bygones', you may say. It would not be accurate to describe this as 'forgetting'. The offended party has not forgotten. 'Pardon' has the same implication as 'forgive'. It suggests that an act has been performed. I spoke of 'rapprochement' but this is not a necessary condition. Neither can we describe this as 'reconciliation'. The offender may be hostile towards the offended and so there is no coming together. So reconciliation is not necessary for this; nor indeed is it a condition of forgiveness. Typically in the break-up of a marriage the parties feel initially hostile towards each other; later, one may come to feel that it is all over and no resentments need remain whilst the other does

---

[19] Norvin Richards, 'Forgiveness', *Ethics* 99 (1988), p. 94, speaks of feelings running their course. The phrase hints at the sort of account I suggest here. Richards is interested in the cases where character complicates the situation and where there may be considerations which make forgiveness not the right option. Behind this I sense another but unarticulated view of forgiveness which is trying to escape and which I try to capture here. Another writer who approaches this view is Richard Holloway in his excellent *On Forgiveness* (Canongate, 2002) (see chapter 3 especially pp. 42 ff). The Hebrew word sometimes associated with our 'forgiveness' is 'salach' which means 'letting go', a phrase used by Geoffrey Scarre in his recent book *After Evil*.

not. There may be forgiveness by one party without reconciliation.

So what do I claim here? It is that the end of anger and resentment comes about in the way that I describe rather than through a willed act of forgiving. The contrary to this is just what is usually contrasted with forgiveness, namely resentment. It is the opposite of both forgiveness conceived as an act and what I described as its alternative. In its worst form it is 'nursing a grudge'. It is a commonplace that bearing a grudge damages the bearer. 'Nursing' a grudge suggests a deliberate nurturing of the resentment. It means keeping it alive by a deliberate reflecting on it, feeding it by constantly returning to it. What I suggest is both that neglect is honourable and that it is more common than an act of forgiveness. Forgiveness as described by Christian thinkers is not a central aspect of our lives nor should it be. It is too officious. Better to allow injuries to fade and resentments to die. What I have described has some of the features we intuitively think of as involved in forgiveness but some, too, are missing. At its best it is an unconsidered process free from striving. Some of us forgive without struggle. There may be those who are naturally nice; they meet injuries and offences with a shrug; they do not take offence. Such people may be sad at an offence against them yet not be angry with the offender. Furthermore for such people forgiveness is not a weapon which can be used to humiliate the offender and establish the moral superiority of the forgiver. For forgiveness is sometimes used in that way; indeed that use is actively encouraged by the Apostle Paul. In counselling against revenge, he writes (Romans 12.20, quoting Proverbs 25) 'Therefore if thine enemy hunger, feed him; if he thirst, give him drink; for in doing so thou shalt heap coals of fire on his head'. (So there!)

But there are offences and offences. The acid test here is how you react to offences committed against somebody else, particularly against somebody you love. If somebody injures your child and you merely feel sad at their wrongdoing, something is wrong. It suggests a detachment which does not reflect well upon you. A proper care and affection for those you love means that you are protective of them and that means that you feel both angry and resentful at their ill-treatment. If you are angry and resentful, as you should be, then it will take time to deal with this and this process of a progressive, developing neglect, is what replaces forgiveness conceived as an act. I have followed Bishop Butler in emphasising resentment. But resentment is not a necessary part of the aetiology of forgiveness, as is often thought. (And resentment seems too small a word for somebody who murdered your wife or child. You would feel impotent rage and fury which might give way to a sort of weary resignation. But resentment smoulders; it is more corrupting in its insidiousness.) The injured person may be angry or contemptuous rather than resentful and forgiveness may involve overcoming these feelings.[20] This may not be as passive a business as I have seemed to suggest. It may involve deliberately avoiding dwelling on the offence. There is a direction of your attention in this case.[21] So does this view of forgiveness rule out the possibility that forgiveness is a virtue?[22] Not at all. Certainly forgiving is not an act. But to have a character which does not dwell on injuries, does not nurture resentment, which tries to understand the history of the woman who has hurt you and which tries to monitor reactions, is to be virtuous in precisely the way that we think of a forgiving man as virtuous. Virtue is a matter of character and need not show itself only in action or in deliberately refraining from action.

The sketch I have offered fits in with an important feature of human forgiveness. The usage 'I have forgiven him' is common and appropriate where 'I forgive you' or 'I forgive him' is not.[23] The first usage may be retrospective to the process of what I have called, rather hesitantly, 'neglect'. The latter are speech-acts and their usage is restricted to minor affronts. I certainly think that that sort of forgiveness

[20] See Richards, *op. cit.*
[21] Compare Paul M. Hughes 'What is involved in forgiving', *Jnl. Value Inquiry* 27 (1993), pp. 331–40.
[22] See Paul M. Hughes, 'What is involved in forgiving' *Philosophia*, vol. 25 (1997), pp. 33–49.
[23] I owe this point to R. Rockingham Gill.

is possible in the context of small offences but, of course, by the same token, it seems either jocular or fairly silly to say 'I forgive you' when somebody unintentionally barges me in a queue or knocks a book out of my hand. These are trivial matters. In the immortal Molesworth tetrology, Fotherington-Thomas, who is, says Molesworth, 'utterly wet and sissy' is a devotee of the cult of Little Lord Fauntleroy. In Molesworth's own words 'when i say he hav a face like a tomato he repli i forgive you Molesworth for those uncouth words'. There is nothing puzzling about Fotherington-Thomas's forgiveness but nothing very weighty either.

Nor can we feel very comfortable about speaking of forgiving children. We cannot rationally resent small children or our pets and we cannot properly speak of forgiving them. They may irritate us and we may then get over it. It is a problem of dealing with children that we have to assume a responsibility for their actions which we know they lack. Were we not to do so they would not grow into people who took responsibility. A parent might say, lightly, like Fotherington-Thomas, 'Mummy forgives you' but it had better not be the weighty business of requiring guilt, repentance and reconciliation it is with adults. To introduce a child to such matters before it is ready can be as damaging as premature sexual contact.

In the experience of two or three people with whom I have discussed this at length, it is the surrogate for forgiveness which I have described as 'neglect' which they have both noticed and experienced. If a notion such as forgiveness is internally inconsistent, seeming to require both an act and a process, (and there is no doubt that some of our concepts, like those of a God who is omnipotent and benevolent, are inconsistent), then it is because these concepts derive from competing requirements and from complex historical antecedents. In my work on the philosophy of art I have suggested that some of the difficulties in the concept of art are the progeny of differing ideological requirements. As I have indicated, my suspicion is that the origins of that notion of forgiveness which is 'theology-laden' are to be found in both Jewish law (which, in as much as it enters the

Christian tradition, is priestly and involved with reparation through sacrifice) and in the Augustinian tradition which places the will at the centre of right action and the notion of forgiving as a willed response.

What I have described has many of the features which we intuitively think of as involved in forgiveness. But some, too, are missing. As I remarked, what I describe may be an unconsidered rather than a consciously sought response to the injury. I suggest we are better if we lack that striving. I also said that the process may be marked by the verdict 'I have forgiven her' without there being any action properly described as that of forgiving. But equally, you may well feel that to say in such circumstances 'I have forgiven' is wrong and misleading. Nothing like forgiveness has taken place. The situation might be simply one described by that wretched word 'closure'. 'We have achieved closure' though not in the way that is normally conceived—by an appropriate punishment. In some cases it is rather that it is now of no great significance to us—though that depends on the scale of the offence. If your linguistic intuitions point this way then I have nothing to add which can persuade you. But by now the differences between us don't matter very much. In your vocabulary I want to replace Christian forgiveness with its emphasis on love and reconciliation by something less weighty. I am rather inclined to call this 'forgiveness' whilst you are not. And that is it.

It needs to be said, too, that on this picture we could not have an obligation to forgive, at least not directly. We may have an obligation to put ourselves into whatever position makes the fading of resentment a more likely outcome—and I shall have something to say about this later. But we cannot have an obligation to do something which we cannot do, and if forgiveness is not an act then we have no obligation to do it. Now Christians certainly do think we have an obligation to forgive and the promptness with which the two ministers in my opening stories forgave suggests as much. I remarked earlier that there may be a precedent for this in 'The Lord's Prayer', though Jesus may there be saying that we should do something more like what I have just proposed — arrange our lives in such a way that resentment will fade.

In this context, one of the more interesting contributions to the debate is that of the pastoral theologian, John Patton, who has diametrically opposite priorities to the other theologian I mentioned, H.R. Mackintosh. Patton is concerned to see how man can forgive. His book is entitled *Is Human Forgiveness Possible?*. His thesis recognises the deficiencies of an analysis which presents forgiveness as an act though the analysis he eventually gives is very far from mine. For one thing he treats forgiveness as univocal and he has no place for what I call 'neglect'. His conclusion is '[H]uman forgiveness is not doing something but discovering something — that I am more like those who have hurt me than I am different from them. I am able to forgive when I discover that I am in no position to forgive'.[24] I mentioned the problem of getting oneself to forgive, or, as I prefer, to 'neglect' or 'cease to harbour' the offence. Patton's proposal is a form of what we might call an 'internal' answer to this question as opposed to an 'external'. Forgiveness comes about by changes in the person who has suffered the offence, enabling him or her to relinquish resentment. The 'external' approach involves considering the forces which brought the offender to do what he or she did. The assumption in this second case is that the injury can be put aside most effectively by concentrating on the causes of the act. When one is able to see what brought the offender to the position where the offence was committed, it is easier to put it to the back of your mind. (I discuss these issues in a later chapter.)

Might we think of forgiveness as an emotion? As the previous discussion suggests, on the whole, I think not. The idea of emotion has been much studied by philosophers in recent years and there is, I think, general agreement on its salient features. Some elements of what is required for an emotion are present in forgiveness. In standard cases of emotion, such as anger, there is an object of anger, the

---

[24] John Patton, *Is Human Forgiveness Possible?* (Abingdon Press, Nashville, 1985), p. 16. Also, see Andrew Gleeson, 'Humanising Evil-Doers'.

offender or the act and there are concomitant beliefs and some judgements of value. Interestingly, pertinent to forgiveness is the thought which is also embodied in anger, that I or somebody else has been injured and that the cause of the injury is a culpable agent and not just a force of nature. Notice that I can be wrong about these. I might be angry with the wrong person, fail to understand that he was not responsible or think I have been injured when I have not. For forgiveness too there are objects (the injury and its perpetrator), beliefs and judgements. In other respects too forgiveness does seem close to emotion. Emotions can catch you unawares. So may forgiveness. Just as you may feel astonishment at your jealousy at a friend's success and disgust with yourself for feeling it, so may forgiveness appear unexpectedly and only be recognised belatedly.

But is there anything here comparable to 'affect'? It is said that pride involves some 'internal swelling' and that anger is reported as an internal 'boiling'. In forgiveness could there be something like an inner warmth? Might you say of somebody you have forgiven, 'my heart goes out to her'? (It was a phrase of my mother's). This is certainly so in Christian forgiveness. But if what I say about 'benign neglect' is correct and if it counts as a form of forgiveness, then this is not a necessary condition. Passionless forgiveness is a possibility. And you might forgive but not want much to do with the offender. You may simply not feel resentment anymore nor wish the offender any ill. Forgiveness may be cold. There need be no reconciliation nor any reaching out to the offender. You might not want his company, either because of what he did or because of what he might do. In any case, such considerations have no purchase at all when the offender was a stranger before and where you will not see him again or, more obviously, if the offender is dead. All in all, though forgiveness may sometimes involve an emotion it does not always and it seems a mistake to think of it as characteristically an emotion.

IV: Can God Forgive?

The Prodigal Son said 'Father, I have sinned against Heaven and in thy sight' (Luke 16.21). It is, I think, not difficult to see that he has offended his father. But why should he have 'sinned against heaven'? Has he offended God as well? The traditional view is that he has. But why?

Theodicies arise to meet the problem of the presence of evil in a world created by a good, and, it is claimed, omnipotent God. The familiar dilemma runs 'Either he can prevent evil but won't; then, where is his goodness; or he wishes to but cannot; then where is his omnipotence?'. But assume the difficulty can be solved either through the free will defence or by some other method. Then if everything we attempt will advance the good we cannot do anything which has bad results. We might attempt to hurt a neighbour but, since all is for the best, he or others will ultimately benefit. Our attempts to act badly are subverted to God's good plans and, in the end, we are impotent. We are frustrated in our attempts to do evil. This holds even for the suicide bombers of 9/11 or the creators of Auschwitz. So, on this understanding what constituted the Prodigal Son's offence against heaven? He could not hurt God, after all, nor in any way frustrate his plans.

Kant thought that if we knew that God would punish or reward every evil or good action the space for moral agency would not exist. If we knew this then prudential considerations would replace acting for the sake of the good.[25] There are reasons not to accept his conclusion but it is true that it is a perpetual temptation to religious believers to substitute prudence for morality. If hell fire awaits the users of condoms, then they will be tempted to avoid condoms not because using them is morally wrong but because it is imprudent. And that is the wrong motive. You may argue that such a temptation can perhaps be resisted; we can ensure that we act because something is good and not because it is to our advantage; perhaps this is so though I

---

[25] See the interesting discussion in Susan Neiman, *Evil in Modern Thought* (Princeton University Press, Princeton. N.J., 2004), pp. 57–84.

think it is often hard to tell on which motive an agent acts and sometimes impossible to disentangle the motive which is operative. There are, in fact two issues here. Firstly, it is hard to see how I can set myself to act from moral motives when both morality and prudence are sufficient conditions for doing something. The second question is this. Once done, how can I or anybody else be sure that the motive I acted on was the right one of the pair? I say this not because I think there is necessarily a truth of the matter which escapes us; that might be the case; but what is equally likely is that there is no fact of the matter here. For in what could such a fact consist?[26] All we have are our reflections, our memories and our behaviour as seen by ourselves and others. If these do not determine an answer as to on which motive I acted, then where is that answer to be found?

In any case, Kant was wrong. There is at least the possibility of an evil will even where the evil action is known to be imprudent. Somebody might, like Verdi's Iago, try to do evil just for the hell of it. Neither are people prudent all the time; the impulse of a moment may make you do something that you know you will later regret. There are bad actions born out of weakness of will. If you subscribe to the theodicy I sketched then the Prodigal Son's crime lay in his intentions not in what he actually brought about.

Whatever your view of all this, a theodicy is already on the rocks. Because in a good world there would be neither ignorance which leads to bad actions nor men capable of weakness of will let alone the existence of people with malign motives. The very existence of evil motives which God subverts to his own good ends shows that the world is not as good as it might be. It would be better without such evil motives in the first place. (I say this in the knowledge that some philosophers think that there is nothing wrong in having bad desires providing they are not acted upon. But I disagree.)

We have imperfect knowledge of the consequences of what we do. Allow that we are stymied by our ignorance of

---

[26] I discussed the 'indeterminacy of the mental' in R.A. Sharpe, *Making the Human Mind* (Routledge, 1990).

the outcome of our actions. We can perhaps guard against the impurity of our motives but we cannot do much to ensure that the good prevails. We can always, through bad luck, find that our best laid plans gang agley. What then might we do to ensure that we act so that we do not harm others? With our imperfect knowledge, the religious believer may tell us that our best course is to obey the One who knows what the outcomes really are. In the words of Hannah 'Talk no more so exceedingly proudly; let not arrogancy come out of your mouth; for the Lord is a God of knowledge, and by him actions are weighed' (I Sam. 2.3.). So it is not very surprising that obedience should be so prominent in religious morality. The assumption is that we can find out what God requires by reading the Bible, or consulting the Vatican or an Imam or a Rabbi. There are experts on what God requires and these are they. Failure to obey God is the original sin. H.R. Mackintosh says that we owe obedience to God and this is our prime duty. So we offend God by the disobedience we attempt. The primary sin here is pride, one of the seven deadly sins.

Now there are difficulties here for modern people. It is hard for us to make obedience such a central virtue. For traditional Christianity it might have been the master virtue; all the other virtues such as compassion and mercy are only required as a consequence; we first must obey God and God requires that we be compassionate and merciful. But we cannot share such a lofty view of obedience. When any virtue becomes less central or even obsolete in a society, it is hard for that society to think of its Deity as exhibiting that virtue or, as in this case, requiring it. Obedience no longer has the role in our society that it once had. Do we require obedience from our children? Only up to the age of majority or thereabouts. The situation where fathers were in a position to dispense patrimony or an estate and made the obedience of their offspring a condition of inheriting it has gone, together with other forms of economic dependence. (In any case their obedience would then be likely to be a matter of prudence.) I may give my children advice but they are under no obligation to take it. The fears I had earlier in my life that whatever money I left them would be spent rapidly on frivolous and temporary satisfactions instead of securing their future has given way to a mixture of optimism and resignation. I cannot make conditions as a paterfamilias might have done in the past. We can, I think, no longer see obedience as a moral requirement; it is a matter of prudence. You obey somebody who knows more about the situation than you do.

Nowadays we think of respect, and of its concomitant obedience, as something which has to be earned. In a hierarchical society like that in which my parents grew up respect was clearly owed to offices. The minister and the teacher were to be respected. They did not have to prove that they were worthy of respect. By and large you did what you were told by these authority figures. As Paul Woodruff observes, unless respect is given rather than earned, society will soon break down.[27] We cannot effectively test the worthiness of all those 'set in authority over us'. Instead, I suggest, respect is defeasible. We withdraw respect when we see it is not merited rather than wait to see whether it is merited before according it.

If obedience becomes less central in a culture, this has ramifications; what we are required to do by our religion may come to be ignored when it clashes with our own consciences. Something like this has happened with the average Roman Catholic's view of contraception. In conversation at dinner once with a prelate from northern Europe I was a little surprised when he remarked to me that he took a very dim view of people from the Vatican poking their noses into his diocese and inquiring whether the flock were using condoms or not.

The idea that we should obey the state is, as well, something we now find problematic. Governments make decisions which are obviously foolish or evidently based on ignorance. We obey them because they impose penalties if

---

[27] Paul Woodruff, *Reverence* (Oxford, 2001), p. 180. Don Cupitt, *The Sea of Faith* (SCM, 1994), ch. 5 is interesting on the intellectual background to the sin of pride which is so closely connected with the sin of disobedience.

we do not. We do not obey them because we think they know better. Examples are legion. In the first years of this new century, the British government has imposed targets in an attempt to motivate hospitals to reduce waiting lists. Because a target was set for cataract operations, the far more serious condition of glaucoma was neglected, with the result that patients had to wait longer for a sight-saving operation. The attention of the authorities was drawn to this to no avail. Possibly they would argue that this was a cost which had to be borne in order to achieve greater goods. More probably they had their eye on the reactions in the media to a statistic recording a reduction in waiting lists. That imposing targets will distort clinical priorities is something that 'any fule kno'—as Molesworth would say. Eye-surgeons do not obey the government because the government knows better what is in the interests of the patients. It is not prudential in that sort of way. It is prudential because otherwise they and their colleagues would suffer by penalties imposed which would hamper in other ways their ability to treat their patients.

Earlier I quoted H.R. Mackintosh as writing that we owe obedience to God. But why should we obey God? What claims has he upon us? Again the Euthyphro dilemma raises its antlers with all its consequent ramifications. We ought to do what we ought to do. To describe such an action as a duty to God adds one thought too many. (I set aside here those other duties which are specifically religious; the requirement of confessions, going to mass, celebrating mass if you are a priest and so on.) Where obedience is required it is required for prudential and not moral reasons. Children should do as they are told because their parents have greater knowledge of the world and of the consequences of their behaviour, good and bad. But once adults, the children may see that the advice given by their parents is foolish.

So, setting aside obligations thought to be required by God—such as daily prayer—and setting aside the question as to whether we should obey God (which is where the Euthyphro dilemma returns) obedience to God could only be required on the basis that God knows best. The problems now are epistemological, as indeed they are in the case of specific religious obligations. How do we know what God expects of us? Because of the conflicts between different religions and sects as to what God requires, it is clear that the majority of proposals as to what God requires must be false. God cannot simultaneously require confession to a priest and a private admission of sin. God cannot simultaneously require that we abstain from blood transfusions, which one sect says he requires, and also not concern himself with the matter, which is what all the other sects think. Nor can he require that we do not use condoms and at the same time, regard their use as permissible. When faith schools teach religion the larger proportion of what they teach must be false.

Interestingly, anyone who believes in a benevolent Deity who imposes obligations on us cannot recognise the existence of moral dilemmas. For him or her there must be a right answer to moral problems. God could not put us in the position of having to choose between two evils because that would make him complicit in the commission of a wrong. But this conflicts with our everyday moral experience. We do face moral dilemmas; we do have to make hard choices and the considerations which make it difficult to choose between them will not disappear just because some priest tells us that God requires us to act in one way rather than the other.

I do not believe that there is a prima facie moral obligation to obey anybody; there is no moral obligation to obey the State and there is no moral obligation to obey God. The best that the State can expect from us is some sense of reciprocity. My philosophical anarchism does not preclude my recognising that I owe the State something. My brand of philosophical anarchism simply denies that I have any prima facie obligations to the State. I owe the State something. It protects me, offers me a health service and educated me. So I am obliged to pay the taxes it levies; for otherwise I would be a free rider. The moral obligations I have to the State are in this sense a bit like contractual obligations though in some ways not. I did not sign up to a contract as an infant. It is because it does something for me that I do my bit for it. But if it ceased to protect me through engaging in foolish foreign military adventures or if it replaced the health service with a private system, then my obligations to it would be restricted.[28] Likewise if I could be sure that God looked after me I might have obligations to him. But when I look around and see the wretched, narrow and poverty-stricken lives lived by other less fortunate people, I put down to luck the fact that my lines have been written in pleasant places. I have spoken as though this is a contract for my benefit only, and the terms of contract theory and the individualism often associated with it naturally suggest that approach. Most contract theorists think this way. But, although I may not personally benefit from the tax regime because I earn more than the average, though my heavy council taxes are not in any way proportionate to the benefits I receive because I have no children of school age, I have no useful local public transport, and although I have not

[28] I will give an example of how this works in practice. The State paid for me to go to University and then gave me a salaried position in which I was able to teach, study and write on philosophy. When I became a senior academic I was frequently asked to act as an external examiner for doctoral and masters' degrees and for undergraduate examinations. The work is considerable and the pay wretched. In 1990 I worked out that I was paid one pound an hour as external examiner for the first degree. For examining a Master's degree the fee at the time of writing is seventy five pounds. This involved two days spent in travelling, and conducting a one hour viva, another 30 minutes or so consultation with the internal examiner and probably 4 or 5 hours reading the thesis. There is no payment for travelling time. Likewise, I readily agreed to act as a referee for articles sent to journals for no pay and gave papers at other universities or at conferences for no fee. This does not reflect particularly well on me. Every academic in my field does the same. All this would be unthinkable in other walks of life, such as the law or business or politics. How long this state of affairs can last when a government replaces an ethos which relies heavily on mutual obligations and reciprocity with one which treats academics as having an infinite amount of time available for the filling in of returns couched in management jargon which is frequently meaningless I do not know. My obligations to do this sort of work became noticeably less stringent as the demand for longer reports on my activities became stronger. The pay did not justify such demands. Ultimately I took on examining as a duty owed to friends, to colleagues and to students rather than as the appropriate activities for an academic.

benefited from the National Health Scheme proportion-
ately to what I have put in because I have been so far fortunate in my good health, nevertheless I support a society
which does things of which I approve for the benefit of
others, even though it does not benefit me.

Back to forgiveness. For traditional Christianity, then,
God forgives us our disobedience. This faces difficulties. If
God forgives us, it must be an act, an exercise of mercy. This
does not mean it is not virtuous; my point is rather that it is
not the same sort of virtue as human forgiveness. Could
God suffer resentment? Can He be enraged? If His feelings
are hurt by the wrong-doing of human beings does it then
make sense to say that this is something he has to get over
before forgiveness can occur? It is not too difficult to think
that the God of the Old Testament and the God of naive
Christians such as many Catholics and most Fundamental-
ists might operate this way but God as conceived by the
more sophisticated probably does not. For intelligent
people do not think of God as lit up by flashes of irritation
let alone an endemic resentment with which He has to
struggle. For human beings forgiveness has a context, a recognition that we who are offended are not without fault,
and an environment which is absent in the Deity.[29]

The gist of this was recognised by Montaigne (and he
recognises the problems it leads him to when wanting to call
Socrates virtuous).

> A man who, from a naturally easy-going gentleness, would
> despise injuries done to him would do something very
> beautiful and praiseworthy; but a man who, stung to the
> quick and ravished by an injury, could arm himself with
> the arms of reason against a frenzied yearning for ven-
> geance, finally mastering it after a great struggle, would
> undoubtedly be doing very much more. The former would
> have acted well: the latter, virtuously; goodness is the word
> for one of these actions; virtue, for the other; for it seems
> that virtue presupposes difficulty and opposition, and can-
> not be exercised without a struggle. This is doubtless why
> we can call God good, mighty, bountiful and just, but we

[29] Compare Downie, op. cit.

cannot call him virtuous; his works are his properties and cost him no struggle.[30]

God forgives us just as the priest bestows forgiveness as an agent of the Church. 'I absolve you' is something done straight off. It is pardon rather than forgiveness, an act rather than the report of a process. It is an exercise of mercy rather as an absolute ruler might let an offender off a penalty. Essentially it is a judicial act. Of course mercy might be a virtue in an absolute ruler. Christianity and Islam unite in thinking that God is merciful (though for some of them it seems that, since it is the job of God to show mercy, it relieves His followers from having to show it). Be that as it may, that God's forgiveness amounts to mercy is consistent with the fact that He could not display the richer, more complex notion of human forgiveness. That cannot be found in a being which does not live the complex life of a human being, with its hurts, vicissitudes and disappointments. Crucial here is the fact that God does not change his attitude towards us. '[W]ith Him there is no variableness neither shadow of turning' (James 1.17). So in the richest sense of forgiveness it is not open to Him to forgive. (A caveat. I assume that it makes sense to speak of God as judging or pardoning. I have a strong presentiment that further thought would show that these claims either have no sense or that they are very marginal or quasi-metaphorical usages parallel to speaking of God as loving or as fatherly. The normal conditions under which it is proper to speak of pardon are so remote from this new context that their sense here is a very exiguous matter indeed. But to show this would take me outside the bounds of this discussion and I must leave it for another book — or another life.)

Other grounds have been offered for objecting to the idea that God can forgive. Firstly, since God always measures judgement according to the offence, he cannot condone or remit the punishment of a peccadillo because this would impugn his justice. Secondly, if forgiveness is the retraction of a judgement about the putative offender which is now

---

[30] Michel de Montaigne, *The Complete Essays*, trans. M.A. Screech (Penguin, 2003), p. 472.

seen to be unjust either because it is based on an error or because the judgement seems too harsh given the scale of the offence, then God, because he does not make such mistaken judgements in the first place, cannot be said to be forgiving in this sense.[31] This second objection, however, seems to me to carry little weight. I question whether forgiveness is the right concept at all here. I can only forgive if the offence is genuine; if anyone is to be forgiven when the judgement is wrong it must be the person who makes the wrong judgement and not the supposed offender.

Some philosophers, notably R.F. Holland and D.Z. Phillips, would not allow that God is part of our moral community.[32] This seems to me to place obstacles in the way of saying that God forgives. The unreflective thought must be that in some ways God is part of our moral community and in some ways not. He does not commit crimes or misdemeanours. He is never rude or thoughtless. These cannot be intelligibly ascribed to God. Yet he forgives. However I rather suspect that, in the end, forgiveness will prove pretty slender when ascribed to a Deity just as ideas of His care for us, or His love for us are rather exiguous. We can understand how language spreads from one central usage to other usages. My work on the philosophy of music discusses how expressive descriptions can move from being used of people to be used of music and vice versa. The problem is that whereas music can be heard and studied, any sense that God can is already far from straightforward. The language game has been moved before we are in a position to move it.

V: Forgiving Oneself

There is a final problem case. R.S. Downie raised the issue of 'forgiving oneself'.[33] We sometimes say 'I cannot forgive

[31] See Anne C. Minas, 'God and Forgiveness', *Philosophical Quarterly* 25 (1975), pp. 138–50.

[32] D.Z. Phillips, *The Problem of Evil and the Problem of God* (SCM, 2004), p. 122 and p. 149.

[33] Downie, op. cit. See also Nancy Snow, 'Self-forgiveness', *Jnl Value Inquiry* 27 (1993), pp.75-80 and Paul M.Hughes, 'On forgiving oneself': a reply to Snow, *Jnl of Value Inquiry* 28 (1994), pp. 557–60.

myself'. But this is in cases where, prima facie, the individual who is injured is somebody else. For the typical case is where you cannot forgive yourself for what you did to somebody else. I qualify it as 'prima facie' because a case can certainly be made out for saying that when you do something bad you injure yourself; as I remarked before, you injure your reputation, you may feel guilt and abhorrence of yourself and you may have set a precedent which makes it easier to commit that offence again. What you did on the spur of the moment seems in retrospect foolish and it damages your confidence in your ability to control yourself in unexpected situations or when you are under stress. You can no longer think of yourself as what Norman S. Care calls an 'in-control agent'.[34] You find yourself stuck with aspects of your personality or behaviour which you may regret or resent. You may even have physically damaged yourself through over-indulgence or through drug-taking. Many cases where self-forgiveness might be at issue are cases where you do something which you feel to be wrong even though nobody else is injured. These may be cases of sexual incontinence or drunkenness or some other form of excess; you may feel guilt over a casual affair where your temporary partner is positively grateful for something she has thoroughly enjoyed and is in no way injured by it; though, of course, many likely cases *are* cases where you injure somebody else.

Nor is anything like resentment involved. I do not resent myself for letting myself down. So self-forgiveness is in some ways untypical of forgiveness generally. Indeed, the central feature here is not that an injury has been done. Where an injury has been done to another, it is for her to forgive you and not for you to forgive yourself. Self-forgiveness is relevant because you feel shame. This is not to be confused with something to which it bears some similarities, and that is embarrassment. I do not think we can be

H.J.N. Horsbrugh, 'Forgiveness', *Canadian Journal of Philosophy* 4 (1974–5), pp. 269–82, see p. 278.

[34] Norman S. Care, *Living with our Past* (Rowan and Littlefield, Lanham MD, 1996), pp. 88–9.

embarrassed in private, so to speak. The commonplace
dreams of being embarrassed at being naked in a public
place are simply due to the fact that everybody else is
clothed and you are both conspicuous and have broken
social conventions just as you might be embarrassed at
turning up to a dinner in a lounge suit only to find everybody else in evening dress (it happened to me once — worse
still, my suit was aubergine and not even subfusc). But you
would not feel embarrassed at being naked on a nudist
beach or, if you were, you would acknowledge that your
embarrassment was irrational. (You would be justified in
embarrassment if you were the only clothed person there.)
Embarrassment involves the public. But shame can be
private. You might be ashamed of your resentful or envious
thoughts about another person even though nobody knows
of them and you do not believe in an all-seeing God.[35]

So how does self-forgiveness come in? You feel you cannot forgive yourself because you have fallen below the standards you set for yourself. You judge yourself and find
yourself wanting. You may feel that you cannot forgive
yourself for having struck your child even though he may
have forgiven you long ago. Now as far as the principal
injury is concerned, what would count as forgiveness here
is a matter already discussed. But what about forgiving
yourself? Let us assume that the question arises because of
the sense that you have injured yourself or let yourself
down. Some people judge themselves very harshly; they
fall below their own high standards. A man may allow that
he has done some good things as well as some bad but that
may not affect his judgement of himself. That is, the ills he
has done always strike him as dreadful and the good things
as trivial, as no more than would be expected of anybody.
He may compare himself unfavourably with somebody
who, though bad-tempered, has devoted her life to helping
others in a way he has not.

Perhaps it is worth contrasting here how one remembers
and how one judges. I remember a relative, now long dead,

---

[35]   See Gabriele Taylor, *Pride, Shame and Guilt* (Oxford University Press,
       1985).

as a pompous man who combined ignorance with arrogance, was a racialist and a bore. But what I remember is not what I judge. In fact he was a kind if rather bad tempered man with a very strong sense of responsibility for those people in the family who had fallen on bad times. That's how I judge him. In the same way, a man who is not self-forgiving may have a tendency to remember what reflects badly on him and that colours his opinion of himself and leads to his low self-esteem. But at the same time his considered judgment may be that he is but 'un homme moyen sensual' and no worse than most. Of those you love and live with, you probably don't make judgements at all. You react to what they say and do, you know how they will respond. You might even know that they can be rude and insufferable to others but you avoid a judgement. Or, perhaps more accurately, the judgement you make does not enter the relationship you have with them. For to make a judgement requires an objective stance which may be hard to reconcile with love.

The woman who feels shame because she has let herself down may feel that she has injured herself by what she has done. Interestingly, 'I cannot forgive myself' is familiar whereas it seems odd for somebody to say 'Yes, I did do that, it was bad, but I have forgiven myself long ago'. (Can you imagine saying 'Yes, I did strangle the chairman of one of the review committees which came to the philosophy department when I taught in it but, fortunately, they did not catch me, it was long ago and, in any case, I have forgiven myself so it's all right now'? — Resist the temptation to say 'Yes'.) The case is asymmetrical with standard cases of forgiveness in what locutions are allowable, but it may not be asymmetrical in terms of the account I give of neglect. Because what I might say about my own offences is parallel to how I regard the offences of others. It was a long time ago — (as Sam Goldwyn reportedly said, 'we have all passed a lot of water in the interim'). To persist in guilt is to be unnecessarily hard on oneself. You may not say 'I have forgiven myself' as you might say of somebody else 'I have forgiven him'. But the procedure is the same. That form of forgiveness which I take to be more significant helps us to deal with this.

Is forgiving oneself linked with loving oneself? Certainly it may be argued that it is easier to forgive somebody you love than somebody you do not — the earlier discussion of William Blake was directed at the difficulty of forgiving friends rather than enemies and the love of friends is not the same as the love of wife, children or parents. So can it be that you can forgive yourself because you love yourself? There is another asymmetry here; the reasons why you forgive yourself ought to be different from those for forgiving somebody you love. You might reason that you must place yourself in the position to forgive a child because you love your child too much for anything to stand between you. The relationship cannot function with continued resentment. Love demands forgiveness.

But the reason for forgiving yourself, on the rare occasion where it happens or is appropriate, is that your guilt makes life harder for others around you. You need to do something about this and you use the methods I have proposed. Harry Frankfurt thinks of self-love as a disinterested concern for oneself.[36] But being concerned about yourself is very different from loving yourself. I may be worried by the prospect of suffering pain and by the knowledge that my suffering will distress my wife. The first concern is primarily for myself but the second is not. Both may exist without my loving myself. Frankfurt says that we rarely seek our own well-being for some other's good. But my example suggests that this is not so.

Recent writers on self-forgiving have concentrated on the way self-forgiveness enables the individual to make a new start, to get on with life and generally to function better. It is assumed that this is a good thing. As the clichés run, we 'draw a line under this', 'move on' and 'start re-building our lives'; (politicians often want to do this without actually admitting that they have done anything wrong). The author of *Wild Swans*, Jung Chang, remarked that all happy people

---

[36] Harry G. Frankfurt, *The Reasons of Love* (Princeton, 2004), pp. 79–80.

are good. The thought seems to be that happiness depends upon feeling good about yourself and feeling bad about yourself not only removes one sine qua non for being a good person but is a positive hindrance. It is certainly easier to act well towards others, to be kind and generous if you feel that life has dealt you a good hand. You have no cause for resentment of others. But this is only part of the story. Certainly I would be a happier old man if I remembered triumphs rather than disasters, successes rather than failures, my kindnesses rather than my resentments and did not feel the curl of embarrassment at my gaffes, remembering rather when I was suave and amusing. But would I be a better person? There may, of course, be a superficial misery rather than a deep and troubling depression which eats at the whole of your life. And if it simply means that the bulk of one's life is spent in a state of self-deprecation and discomfort, your ability to run your life may not be affected. But it may. If self-forgiveness removes these features from your life, contrary to what has been suggested, it may not be a good thing. It may help us to function better, it may be self-rehabilitating but the cost may be more than we ought to pay. There is a case to be made for misery and unhappiness and low self-esteem.

VI: Conclusion

My conclusion is that there are thicker and thinner senses of 'forgiveness'.[37] Firstly there is that which combines a deliberate attempt to neutralise resentment with both attention to the offence and perseverance in trying to clear up the estrangement which has occurred. I described this as Christian forgiveness and love for others plays a central role here. Secondly, and thinner, there is what I describe as 'benign neglect'. Thirdly there is the sense in which Princess Elizabeth might have forgiven the regicides, wishing them no

---

[37] Many concur on the existence of several forms of forgiveness. See, for example, Christopher Bennett, 'Personal and Redemptive Forgiveness', *European Journal of Philosophy*, 11 (2003), pp. 127–44 and Geoffrey Scarre, op. cit. Compare John Kekes, *The Morality of Pluralism* p. 9.

further harm but not looking for reconciliation. Finally, and thinnest of all, there is the sense in which God forgives us through an act of pardoning — in a quasi-legal way. Such remission can only be given by a person or being in a certain relation of authority over the offender. A difference between the Christian and myself would be that he attaches great moral weight to the first whereas I think it might very well amount to fussiness. It is the second form which I endorse and I remain a little unclear as to whether this counts as forgiveness. My unclarity about this may very well be an accurate perception of unclarity in the concept itself; it simply is not fully articulated. No one of the four cases described above seem to me to represent the paradigm or central case of forgiveness.

What the Christian religion does is to expand the concept of forgiveness so that what once was appropriate in a relatively narrow area is thought to apply quite generally. The move is from the assumption that what is right in some cases, to forgive and to restore a damaged relationship, is always proper. One can see this in Butler's seminal work on forgiveness.[38] Butler writes

> … without knowing particulars, I take it upon me to assure all persons who think they have received indignities or injurious treatment, that they may depend upon it, as in a matter certain, that the offence is not as great as they themselves imagine. We are in such a peculiar situation that we can scarce any more see them as they really are, than our eye can see itself. If we could place ourselves at a due distance, i.e. be really unprejudiced, we should frequently discern that to be in reality inadvertence and mistake in our enemy, which we now fancy we see to be malice or scorn. From this proper point of view, we should likewise in all probability see something of these latter in ourselves, and most certainly a great deal of the former.

Butler seems to have forgotten the terrible deeds of the Thirty Years War or the English Civil War. Had he remembered these surely he would not have been so dismissive. What is striking is that the cases he takes are, by implication, small scale offences. We would not argue thus about the

---

[38] Joseph Butler, *Sermon IX* 'Upon Forgiveness of Injuries'.

actions of Martin Borman or Mendele. It is small offences which can be forgiven in the richer sense which I have attributed to Christian thought. The actions of monsters of depravity like Stalin or Pol Pot can only be forgiven in the sense that we may wish that no further harm befall these men than the harm they have already done to themselves by their cruelty to others.

Chapter Three

How to Forgive

Now that we have some idea of the various forms that forgiveness can take, we might ask how, given that being forgiving is a virtue, such a virtue can be nourished. How do I
set myself to forgive somebody who has offended me? The
question arises for more than one form of forgiveness; it
does not arise so directly for 'benign neglect'; there you
merely try not to dwell on matters. But, even in this case, it
may be difficult not to wish to harm the offender. Certainly
getting myself to forgive is problematic when it comes to
Christian forgiveness. How do we learn to love our enemies
and those who despitefully use us?

I shall distinguish two main ways, the first is by attending
to the offender and seeing that there is more to her than
those aspects of her character which produced the offence.
The second is by attending to the offence itself. In this
second case I may be able to forgive her via the way I explain
what she has done. I see that she was under stress or the
victim of forces she could not easily counter. I may see her as
less responsible than I thought. Now I shall point out that
both modes of explanation are less exculpatory than is often
thought. There is a tendency to conflate explaining and
excusing. It is often assumed that to explain is to show that
the offence is not so bad as was thought. But both modes of
explanation can have the contrary effect. When I find out
more about the offender I might discover that she is nasty in
a variety of ways and this offence was, by her standards,
comparatively mild. Or, in the second case, understanding
her action can show that the offence was *worse* than I first
thought so that the only form of forgiveness left open to me

is the minimal. I wish her no further harm. I refuse to look for revenge.

Let's start with a fundamental matter left over from the previous discussion and which is implicit in the distinction I have just drawn. Do we forgive actions or do we forgive people? This will probably strike the layman as a typically philosophical piece of nit-picking. One is inclined to say 'both'; we forgive people and we forgive actions; and that would be right, of course. But, as we shall see, nit-picking can forestall further entanglements and infestations. For there is a broad distinction between thinking of forgiveness as directed at an offence and forgiveness as directed at somebody. If forgiveness is primarily thought of as directed at people much of what Kolnai described as the 'paradoxy' in the concept disappears. It will no longer be true that to the extent you understand the action it ceases to be an action for which forgiveness or non-forgiveness is appropriate; for that carries the suggestion that to the extent you see the action as being done under pressure or in partial ignorance, in ignorance of its consequences or of what occasioned it; to that extent the agent is not fully responsible. Rather, on the view that it is the agent who is forgiven, forgiveness requires that we see the action in a context and the context is that there are other sides to the offender. The offender may be also a good father or good son. He may show loyalties which, in anger at the offence, you do not consider. In doing this we are seeing aspects of the agent which lie beyond the act alone. It is inevitable then that many of the problems of the topic are less in evidence when we take this alternative. As I say, we think of the offender as not wholly bad, as having other sides to his character and his offence as perhaps untypical. Perhaps we will now think that his action was to be expected of somebody with such passionate commitments just as his subsequent remorse could have been expected too. He may have been rude to you because you irritate him; his dislike of you might be quite unjustified; but in many other ways and to other people he is kind and helpful. We forgive without the risk of merely condoning the offence; we are not overlooking a wrong in the process or in any way waiving the appropriate punishment. In such cases repentance aligns the offender with the victim. We share human weaknesses with the offender and cannot afford to stand on our high horses. Consequently, we can see how forgiveness can be accelerated by understanding. We might say 'there, but for the grace of God, go I'.[1]

To insist that it is the act which is the primary focus of forgiveness would be to allow something like the following. I might say 'I forgive the shooting of my cat but I don't forgive the shooting of my wife'. (This is as close as I can get to speaking as though no agent were involved or speaking as though the agent played no part in the moral assessment.) If locutions which omit reference to the agent were possible then it might seem as though a case could be made out for forgiving acts rather than agents. But we don't talk this way and that is significant. We surely would rather say 'I could perhaps have forgiven him for shooting my cat but I cannot forgive him for shooting my wife' and the nature of that locution makes it fairly clear that those thinkers who believe that it is people who are forgiven (or not) for what they do are correct. We can hate the sin and love the sinner. Indeed the grammar of forgiveness (using 'grammar' in its proper sense and not in the sense used by Wittgenstein and his followers) makes the nature of forgiveness clear. It is a three-term relationship. X forgives Y for Z. If you merely say 'I forgive Dennis', we will ask 'What for?'

Butler seems to concur with the idea that forgiveness registers those other dimensions of a man's life not implicated in the offence; 'the resentment could surely at least be confined to that particular part of the behaviour which gave offence: since the other parts of a man's life and character stand just the same as they did before.'[2] But this is wrong in at least two ways. Firstly it is not the case in other than trivial offences that a man's life always stands as it was. An offence

---

[1]   Andrew Gleeson makes this awareness of our common vulnerability to committing evil crucial in understanding how people guilty of great crimes may nevertheless belong to our moral community, sharing our common humanity.

[2]   Joseph Butler, *Sermon IX*, para 16.

is corrosive. A good man will regret what he has done. But it is not always just a case of a shocked 'What have I done?' (as Raymond Gaita so effectively puts it);[3] it may also be an equally shocked 'I am capable of that!' just aside from any effect it has on the trust of others. And it may set a precedent. Vivisectionists probably start off feeling appalled by the suffering they cause. But their lecturers and professors insist that this is what is to be done and eventually they get used to it. It then ceases to worry them. They find justifications. Humankind, they tell themselves, will benefit from what they are doing. No doubt this is what happens as well to people who torture. Even if people are not inured to wickedness by doing wrong, it remains the case, as I argued in the last chapter, that I am harmed by what I do even if I only do it once. The obvious conclusion is that what we do and what we are cannot be so sharply separated.

Agree, then, that you forgive *people* for their actions. The offender has a personality which displays itself in the various things she does, good as well as bad, sometimes under pressure and sometimes not. She has a character and the character expresses itself in various ways. Now a common assumption is that there is a heart to your character. Commonly people talk about 'finding themselves' and perhaps they think of this as discovering the essential 'me', though they rarely stop to ask whether there is such a thing and whether they would like it if they found it. There is a distinction between one's basic character, largely inherited, I think, but perhaps including some aspects added by the accretion of interests later on, and what we do. As Larkin's famous poem points out, we derive our character very largely from our parents. I see aspects of my dead mother and father in my own character, in my dispositions to behave and in my mannerisms as well as my looks. Often what irritates you about yourself is what irritates you about your parents and your children. Adopted children are salutary in that respect. The needling of what you see in your

---

[3]   Raymond Gaita, *Good and Evil; An Absolute Conception* (MacMillan, 1991).

own child is not present. Sometimes you can more easily love their characters, sometimes, of course, not.

This is not a technical work of philosophy and is not the place to debate how Professor X differs from Professor Y. Nevertheless it might be worth mentioning that some philosophers think that a discussion in terms of character is a basic error. There is no such thing as character, they claim. In support of this they adduce empirical research. The idea is that just as philosophers distinguish 'folk physics' from 'scientific physics' or, more debatably, 'folk psychology' from a more sophisticated approach to mentality, so we may distinguish 'folk morality' from a critical morality. Thus intuitively we might say of two balls dropped from a tower that the heavier one will fall more quickly or that a heavy object dropped from an aeroplane will fall to earth in a straight line; in fact both suppositions are false and can be shown to be false. In the same way some have argued that our concepts of mind which express themselves in talk of motive, emotion, belief or intention will be replaced with other concepts such as those of neurophysiology, through the development of science. Similarly, rather than explaining the behaviour of other people in terms of character traits, we should be explaining them in terms of differing perceptions of the situations they find themselves in. Character explanations are frequently inaccurate.[4]

---

[4]   See Gilbert Harman. 'Moral Philosophy meets Social Psychology: Virtue Ethics and the Fundamental Attribution Error', *Proceedings Aristotelian Society* Vol. XCIX (1999), pp. 315–31. An antidote to this implausible thesis can be found in John Keke's admirable and wise book *Facing Evil* (Princeton University Press, 1990). Notably, a widely cited source on this, Lee Ross and Richard E. Nisbett, *The Person and the Situation; Perspectives of Social Psychology* (Temple University, Philadelphia, 1991) is quite cautious, admitting that attribution theory (which ascribes behaviour to underlying character) fits ordinary cases satisfactorily but fails when we try to predict how people will respond to the exceptional. But this is not really very surprising. I suppose we might opt for an instrumentalist theory on this, treating character as a useful predictive and explanatory fiction. The problem here is that I do not know what a more robustly realist account than this would amount to. There can hardly be real things such as character somehow inspectable in the brain.

Firstly, the thesis seems a thesis in the philosophy of mind rather than in moral philosophy, in as much as the two can be kept apart (which philosophers of this ilk generally believe, anyway). In fact conceived as a thesis in moral philosophy it would be rather strange. The Galilean physicist can appeal to facts to demonstrate that intuitive ideas about falling bodies are wrong. But what comparable 'moral facts' could a revisionist moral philosopher appeal to? We have not been told. The second objection is that to replace talk of character with talk of the way in which we attribute differing perceptions to differing people is question-begging. The difference between somebody who treats others as threats and somebody who treats others as friendly and innocuous unless he has reason to think otherwise is simply the difference between the suspicious character and the generous-hearted.

The fact is that the character of others dictates how we deal with them. When I was head of a philosophy department I quickly learnt to send all circulars from the University which required a departmental response to one lecturer before the others, for I knew that otherwise his comments would only relate to what the last respondent had said (he would disagree with him and, if it was possible, with all the previous respondents) and not with the issues at all. It was an aspect of his character.

Anybody who breeds cats and dogs will see the character coming out in generation after generation, sometimes skipping a generation, sometimes revealing a character belonging to some ancient progenitor. I was rather forcibly made aware of the fundamental nature of character when, as a teenager, I put my hand down to stroke a litter of Siamese kittens. Of these, all with eyes just open, all but one were docile and affectionate. One spat at me. A kitten to be wary of. Now you might argue that the range of character in animals is too restricted for the claim to be other than trivial. Ancestors and descendants will resemble each other in character because the range is so limited. In fact, I think that dogs, in particular, are complicated enough for it to be a non-trivial matter. You may find strikingly different characters within the same litter. Whatever the case, it is evidently true of human beings both that character is inherited and that it may vary widely between siblings. I also accept that it can be modified by will-power or by social setting but only, I suspect, within limits.

There is a much more sophisticated form of scepticism about character than the form we discussed earlier in connection with 'attribution theory' and the presumption of a folk morality. This more plausible approach amounts to a sort of non-realism about character. The idea is that we 'construct' the characters of others through the way we interpret their behaviour. The claim of 'non-realism' may suggest that they do not 'really' have the character they are supposed to have. Indeed, it might be supposed that they have no character at all, and that would amount to a form of scepticism about character of precisely the form we rejected. But the theory need not maintain this. It is more plausible to suppose that we act up to the roles we are allotted and act in accordance with the way we are expected to act. Rather than other people recognising the character we have, the character we have is dependent on what people believe they recognise in us. We are, after all, social animals and it matters both to us and to other people that we behave predictably; we make sure that their predictions come true. Something of this appears in a familiar feature of humankind. Most of us are aware that we behave differently in different contexts and with different people. Amongst some academics, I used to feel a bit like a second hand car salesman, extroverted and humorous — amongst others the very epitome of a desiccated academic.

Proust, writing of Swann, says

> But then, even in the most insignificant details of our daily life, none of us can be said to constitute a material whole, which is identical for everyone, and need only be turned up like a page in an account-book or the record of a will; our social personality is a creation of the thoughts of other people. Even the simplest act which we describe as 'seeing someone we know' is to some extent an intellectual process. We pack the physical outline of the person we see with all the notions we have already formed about him,

and in the total picture of him which we compose in our minds those notions have certainly the principal place. In the end they come to fill out so completely the curve of his cheeks, to follow so exactly the line of his nose, that each time we see the face or hear the voice it is these notions which we recognise and to which we listen. And so, no doubt, from the Swann they had constructed for themselves my family had left out, in their ignorance, a whole host of details of his life in the world of fashion, details which caused other people, when they met him, to see all the graces enthroned in his face and stopping at the line of his aquiline nose as at a natural frontier.[5]

But we cannot take this picture at face value. There are limits on my behaviour beyond which I cannot go . We are not merely the product of those around us. Though we are moulded, something of our initial form resists very radical change.

We recognise, as well, that we can make mistakes about others and the mistakes we make may have repercussions when it comes to forgiveness. I may censure another only to learn of the immense pressures she was under. Perhaps she had suffered a recent bereavement or was feeling ill and this caused her to snap. Or perhaps I did not realise that I had touched on a particularly sensitive matter. Suppose I forgive somebody only to find either that the other aspects of her character which I had thought ameliorating did not exist. She is worse than I supposed. Do I then cancel my forgiveness? Have I been foolish? Much the same applies when we consider how the explanation of her actions, and the pressures on her are to be taken into account—the second way in which forgiveness can be advanced. I may, again, be mistaken.

Part of our Christian legacy is that many of us prize innocence. We think it better to be taken in and forgive rather than to be suspicious and not forgive. If forgiveness depends upon honourable illusions, it is not thereby invalidated. In fact, if I am right about the influence of Christianity on the way we think, this process of forgiveness leads

[5]   Marcel Proust, Swann's Way. Overture, *Remembrance of Things Past*, trans. C.K. Scott Moncrieff and Terence Kilmartin (Penguin, Harmondsworth, 1989), p. 20.

inexorably in the direction of 'benign neglect'. Once we have forgiven, then too much time has elapsed to recommence a vendetta. It would be beneath me to bother. If I were mistaken and the offender was worse than I thought, that is sad, but it is not a reason to withdraw forgiveness. In practice we often think it right to avoid double jeopardy and think it wrong to re-open old wounds.

As I have hinted, to some extent what philosophers call 'essentialism' is hard to avoid when thinking about character. It is a feature of our understanding of ourselves. There is a core to the personality, a character. We have both centre and periphery. It is also an essential ingredient in our ability to get on with others. 'She isn't really like that', you say, 'She isn't well' or 'She is flustered' or 'She is having a bad time' etc. There are pressures on her which make her act against the grain. This enables us to bracket those moments of stress and unease which produce reactions which are untypical and perhaps unpredictable. It is important to us that we can do this if the person concerned is a friend, a colleague or a member of the family. We need to get on together and a distinction between a particular action and character in general is a critical tool in this. This is why forgiveness is so important. With a stranger there is no such commitment to be preserved and so perhaps one does not have to extenuate.

So, despite what Blake said, forgiveness is sometimes more easily achieved where there is an existing relationship with the offender. This is what we would have predicted given that we forgive people for what they do and not their actions alone. If somebody you know says or does something offensive you can measure it against your experience that she is, in general, kindly and helpful. It makes it possible to see this offence as an aberration and as therefore forgivable.[6] But, of course, by the same token it may be less easy to forgive. You can be injured by somebody you normally get on well with when he suddenly turns on you. You are hurt by the impatience of somebody to whom you are close in a way that is not possible if the individual who is

---

[6]   See Piers Benn, 'Forgiveness and Loyalty', *Philosophy* 71 (1996), pp. 369–83.

rude is a stranger. You expected something different from a friend and this, of course, confirms the general thesis, that forgiveness and non-forgiveness are especially relevant within an existing relationship.

However, it has been argued more strongly that it is only possible in such cases; that if somebody I have not seen before and never see again steps on my foot and apologises, it cannot be said that I either forgive or do not forgive her. For the condition which makes forgiveness possible is absent, a relationship. But this seems hard to accept. The relationship caused by the encounter may be exiguous in the extreme but it has the minimum necessary for forgiveness to be possible. They may be strangers but they are still people. Perhaps the forgiveness here is no more than a formality, a piece of etiquette. It can hardly be forgiveness in the rich Christian sense. But we need not baulk at calling it 'forgiveness'. It is part of the argument of this book that forgiveness comes in thicker and thinner varieties.

One way of distinguishing character from those individual, incidental actions which may or may not be characteristic of the person in question is to contrast reactions, on the one hand, from considered responses on the other. Unless I am forewarned I tend to act mildly when somebody is rude to me, part of my character, perhaps. But I have noticed that some others are immediately aggressive when crossed. Does reaction show the real personality? There is a temptation to think so; matters may be made a little more complex in as much as your personality may be a consequence of a decision to let your reactions follow, so to speak. You make no effort to guard your character. You might deliberately relinquish control in the interests of spontaneity; this could, of course, be a good or a bad thing. It may also be a matter of debate as to which actions are the freer actions. Are they the spontaneous actions or are they those which are the product of deliberation? Does deliberation suggest constraints, even if the constraints are self-imposed? And if we can identify the actions which are free, have we then picked out the actions which are truly self-revelatory? To put it into contemporary vernacular, 'which is the real you?'

You might then think that an action which flows directly from that character is such that the question of forgiveness cannot even arise. But this is not so; we can and do condemn somebody who acts in character if we believe that he should have made some attempt to resist it or have placed himself out of the reach of temptation. We neither forgive nor fail to forgive a man for his character because his character is not directly in his control; but we might not forgive somebody who makes no attempt to guard against his failings or takes no steps to try to bring about changes in his character. So the relationship between forgiveness and character is in fact complicated. Do we more readily forgive those who act badly but out of character? It depends, to some extent, on the scale of the crime, of course. We might feel that somebody of evil character, who takes pleasure in persecuting others without having any conscience about the matter, might be a different case from somebody who deliberately stills qualms of conscience. The latter corrupts his own initially good character. Indeed it could be argued that the latter individual is the worse of the two.[7] There are interesting questions here about the difference between setting aside the bad action of an otherwise good man and crediting an evil man with an occasional act of kindness and I intend to discuss these in a little while. But first we need to attend to some more general questions about character and identity.[8]

In the analytic tradition of philosophy, identity has been variously thought of as a matter of bodily integrity and continuity on the one hand and psychological persistence on the other. The tradition runs from Locke onwards and is very familiar. The problems are genuine enough but a concentration on this issue to the neglect of other ways of conceiving identity has had a malign effect, a tendency to detach the self from the desires we have and the aims and purposes which we choose; it is as though the ends I have

[7]   See Daniel Haybron, 'Evil Character', *American Philosophical Quarterly* 36 (1999), pp. 131–48. Also relevant here is Bernard Williams. 'Persons, Character and Morality' in *Moral Luck* (Cambridge University Press, 1981).

[8]   For a valuable historical survey, see J.W. Burrow, *The Crisis of Reason* (Yale, 2000), chs. 3, 4 and 5.

are ends I own rather than features which characterise me. The self therefore shrinks to a dimensionless point, a chooser of means and ends and the owner of beliefs and desires. Over the last twenty years or so another and richer notion of identity has entered the fray, a notion implicit in talk of creating or discovering an identity. We are partly constituted by the environment in which we grow up, the religion, ideology, nationality and family ties which give us values which we do not choose. To these we should add a third feature and that is *character*. Consider the following list.

Charm, intelligence, humour, imagination, quick-wittedness, insecurity, bitterness, courage, companionableness, fastidiousness, suavity, politeness, sanguinity, melancholy, acrimony, passion, volatility, malice, vanity, rigidity, pride, selfishness, obduracy, exuberance, quick-temperedness, vulnerability, caution, adventurousness, reticence, acerbity, constancy.

Some of these may be virtues and some vices, and it may be a little hard to say which. But all describe character and the character may be hard to change and not always acquired in the way that communitarian features of identity are acquired, that is through growing up in a specific culture. Many of those I listed we may describe as 'deep features' and this carries just that suggestion that they resist change. 'Character' may be best understood, then, as an amalgam of inherited dispositions and communitarian elements without excluding the possibility that some features have been gathered in other ways — through the slings and arrows of fortune, the accidents that befall us, whether fortunate or unfortunate, and through the choices we have made.

I have distinguished between your character and what you do. As we have seen, it is plausible to suppose that character is crucial to the concept of forgiveness in as much as the difference between what we do and who we are allows the slack for at least one form of forgiveness; forgiveness enters at that point. Of course, the distinction is not clearly marked because what you do shows what you are; but although the former is a proper indicator of the latter, I want to allow that people can act out of character and the idea of acting out of character raises some interesting further questions.

II

Earlier I touched on the question of asymmetry. Is there an asymmetry between the good acts of a bad man and the bad acts of a good woman? Might it be that acting out of character is forgivable in a good woman whereas there is no parallel way of assessing the solitary or infrequent good actions of an otherwise bad man? I shall conclude, and readers will not be very surprised, that there is no general answer. Sometimes the cases are symmetrical though more often, I suspect, not. One relevant thought is this; the 'natural' response to an offence against me is resentment whereas the 'natural' response to a good turn done is (and ought to be) gratitude. Should I then feel gratitude to the bad man who, unexpectedly (since I know him), does me a good turn? As a matter of fact we often do not feel gratitude when somebody who is generally selfish is unexpectedly kind. 'About time, too' is the usual response. There will also be an element of puzzlement. 'What brought that about ?' we may ask. In addition we often suspect the motive of somebody who does us, unexpectedly, a good turn when we know him to be basically selfish. If there is a suggestion that the person concerned is reforming then matters are different, a situation which can be mirrored when the good woman takes a turn for the worse. But, one might argue, if we look for extenuating circumstances when somebody basically good is unexpectedly nasty, then we have some sort of symmetry here. Because if we try to reconcile a woman's bad act with the fact that we know or believe her to be basically good, then we follow a parallel course when we try to find the malicious motive behind an apparently decent act by a person we know or believe to be a nasty customer. To this extent, there seems no prima facie reason to deny symmetry even though we have no single word which covers 'cancelling' gratitude in the way that forgiveness 'cancels' resentment, although I have suggested that in respect of gratitude and resentment the cases do differ.

We need an example. There is a passage in Proust which has fascinated me for years. It tells against the picture I have just limned. The Verdurins have a salon and they resent any of their clientele deserting them for a rival gathering. They are presented, as Proust tends to display bourgeois society, as ignorant, snobbish and their culture as utterly superficial. Mme. Verdurin has no understanding of the music she affects to respond to. In particular they treat one of their proteges consistently badly, humiliating him on occasion and mocking him. Yet when a failure on the stock market reduces him to penury, the narrator over-hears them, thinking they are alone, deciding to do what they can to help him in adversity. Proust concludes that one can never anticipate the good even bad people are capable of; the implication seems to be that one should not judge. But what does this solitary act of sympathetic understanding tell us about the Verdurins? The subtlety of Proust comes out in his avoidance of the suggestion that the Verdurins are exploiting their power over another; their motivation is decent and the act is deliberate and not on whim. This is rare. Proust displays a remarkable generosity in the way he describes the Verdurins.

What is interesting in this case is the connection with principled behaviour. I don't know whether the Verdurins' actions are principled or not. Generally, we think of the good woman as principled and the bad man as not for we rarely think of a bad man as acting badly from principle. Does this mean that we think his actions are the consequence of a lack of control over his violent and selfish propensities? Not necessarily; a bad man may be whimsical in his crimes. He may not act on the basis of any deep-seated tendency and so he may also be whimsical in his acts of benevolence; we also tend to credit him with selfish motives on the latter occasions; thus we might well think that the glow of self-congratulation which the bad man feels on doing something good, helping an old lady or a child, is itself the motive for which he does that thing. We often presume a kind of immature shallowness about the wicked. Consequently we have no reason to find extenuations for the crime or to forgive him. We may not have any need to keep alive any relationship of affection and trust; that may have long ceased to be a consideration so there is again no precise symmetry with the requirements which make us ready to set aside the mistakes of an otherwise good person. Nor do we think that his good action is brought about by pressure that he cannot resist — which is what we assume to be the case when a good woman acts badly. With somebody who is evil, who takes pleasure in harming others, his unexpected act of kindness or generosity may sometimes be put down to a desire to keep others on the hop. Both his bad acts and his good acts may be the result of whimsy whereas we think of a good woman as habitually kind or even as principled in her kindness. Her bad actions come from weakness and not whim. It seems that, at least in these respects, the cases are, in the end, usually asymmetrical.

I said that a good woman may be principled in her kindness. Let me expatiate. In the case of virtues, there is frequently, at least in humans, a valuing of a virtue by the woman who exercises it. She thinks that it is a good thing to possess this particular virtue. For example, she may very well rank the virtue of prudence, which she possesses, higher than other virtues which she does not possess. However I suspect that a vicious man does not normally think of his vices in that way. He probably does not reflect on them much at all for only a few bad men would exercise their vices accompanied by the thought 'This is required of me'. When somebody is like that are we inclined to think he or she has a perverted conception of the good? Consider the difference between Verdi's (or Boito's) conception of Iago and Shakespeare's. In Shakespeare, Iago conveys the disorderly nature of evil; he is an agent of chaos, destructive rather than counter-constructive. The sense that evil and chaos are connected is present. In Shakespeare, Iago, as Victor Hugo perceptively remarked, is unable to bear any superiority. His motive is envy; Samuel Johnson thought that envy was the worst of vices for the envious woman gained nothing through harming the person she envied. But in Verdi's *Otello* Iago expresses in his Credo, a counter-vision of the good.

I said that characteristically we will think of the good person as principled and the bad person as not. Verdi's Iago is an exception; he is bad and makes a principle of his badness. If he acts well he acts out of weakness. Were he to act well, then it might lead us to modify our impression of him. He is not so bad after all, we think. Consider another example. The principled racist finds himself moved by the predicament of a black child and, despite himself, he helps it. He then despises himself for his weakness. We, however, 'count it unto him for righteousness' (to use the lovely Biblical phrase).[9] If this is so, then there are circumstances where the two cases appear symmetrical in a way which we previously discountenanced.

I have made rather extensive, though not exhaustive, use of the distinction between acting on principle and acting on whim. There are also cases, like that I have just described, which fall into neither category. The racist who is moved to help a black child does not act on whim. He has a reason for doing so. Rather, it is, for example, the tyrant who spares one man but condemns another for no reason and for no motive other than exercising his arbitrary power, who acts on whim. Again we should note that we cannot equate acting on whim with those actions for which we have no reasons. I may decide on whim to go for a walk. The precise path I take across the field also has no reason behind its selection. Yet I do not call that a matter of whim. Bernard Williams was once asked about evil and described a politician who, when bored, spread malicious tales about others just for something to do. The point here is that it proceeded not even from envy but from an uncontrolled whim — neither corrected by any overall system of values nor motivated by the desire to bring about some end. The anecdote

---

[9] The reference to Abraham believing and it being counted unto him for righteousness recurs in the Bible see Gen. 15.6, Rom. 4.3. and Gal. 3.6. See Ps. 106.31 as well.

catches perfectly the capricious nature of tyrants who terrify by their unpredictability, one moment torturing somebody who speaks out, the next showing unexpected generosity or even sentimentality. Of course, tyrants need not be like this. Hitler had a perverted notion of the good; he is closer to Verdi's Iago. Stalin was, it seems, more a capricious tyrant who could be entertained by stories of the terror of his victims.[10]

Aside from all this, something needs to be said about actions which seem to flow from the person you are and actions which do not. One way of making sense of this is to distinguish between those desires which are intrinsic and those which are extrinsic. Suppose you are surprised by a sudden appetite for a particular food or that you suddenly become interested in something which has never interested you before. Would it be right to think of this as an extrinsic interest? It might, after all, disappear as suddenly as it arrived and we would be non-plussed both by its appearance and its disappearance. You might be struck with a sudden infatuation for a totally unsuitable woman. A middle-aged woman might be smitten, unexpectedly, with lust for a young man and feel that the emotion is both shaming and ridiculous. It would be natural to think of this as extrinsic. It is not characteristic of her. A friend knew a man with paedophiliac tendencies which he described to her as 'his problem'. This seemed to both of us a fairly transparent attempt on his part to externalise a desire which he regretted. Self-deception seems in the offing. Just how intrinsic to his personality was his desire? Did he fantasise regularly? Did he manoeuvre himself into positions where he could meet children? Or did he avoid jobs which brought him into contact with them?

---

[10] Some of these ideas appeared in my 'Character, Conversion and Identity', in K.S. Johanessen and T. Nordenstam eds., *Wittgenstein and the Philosophy of Culture* (Holder-Pichler-Tempsky 1996), The Proceedings of the 1995 Wittgenstein Symposium in Kirchberg, pp. 232–43. I learnt from O.Flanagan and A.O Rorty eds., *Identity, Character and Morality, Essays in Moral Psychology* (Bradford, MIT, 1990). M.J. Sandel, *Liberalism and the Limits of Justice* (Cambridge University Press, 1981) influenced me heavily.

This whimsical form of wickedness seems not to fall into any of the categories which are the traditional subject matter of the philosophical analyst. For example, we can distinguish somebody who acts wickedly through having bad preferences or bad values from somebody who overrides moral considerations in acting for his own interests; the latter thereby displays a lack of moral concern for the interests of others; yet a third category is exemplified by somebody who is akratic or weak-willed, failing to show self-control. But the person whose acts are arbitrary or chaotic or based on whim may not be deliberately acting so as to keep others on the hop and his own interests may certainly not be furthered thereby. And, as I have said, it is unusual indeed for such a person to be bad out of principle.[11]

Acton remarked somewhere 'we judge a great criminal by the worst of his crimes'. What I have said here tends to endorse that, at least to the extent that we allow little room for anything to be said in favour of the bad man. We excuse the evil-doing of an otherwise good man but tend not to find much to the credit of a bad man even if what he does is on occasion meritorious. This question of principle is central here. It is because good people are usually principled in their goodness whilst bad people are not generally principled in their badness that the entire issue arises. The question which then follows is whether an uncharacteristic action can redeem or blight a life. Could an act of heroism or saintliness redeem an otherwise wretched life? Conversely could a single unpredicted crime blight an otherwise blameless existence? The question cannot be answered in the abstract. It depends upon the scale of the act of heroism in the first case and the converse in the second. It would not be difficult to invent examples of which one would be inclined to say that the action does redeem or blight as the case may be.

Is the converse of Acton's dictum true? Do we judge a good man by the best of his actions? I am not sure. A good person is consistently good and there is no reason to pick

---

[11] See Ronald Milo, *Immorality* (Princeton, 1984), see p. 28 for example.

out an especially good action as typical. Parenthetically the analogy does carry through to the area where we make judgements about value on a more routine basis, the arts; we may well judge a poet by the finest of his poems. A journalist recently described Dylan Thomas's poems as 'Welsh windbaggery' (a description which, as an Englishman settled in Wales, I object to as racist) but he then described *Under Milk Wood* as a comic masterpiece (which it is). But his overall judgement of Thomas as a writer of little talent surely cannot be sustained in the light of his judgement of *Under Milk Wood*. If a poet produces something as good as that, then he is a writer of great talent.

III

The second way in which forgiveness may come about is through understanding the antecedents of the action. How could one forgive a concentration camp guard or a Palestinian suicide bomber? How does one set about doing it? We may look into the forces which made him act that way as distinct from the forces which made him the man he became, the religious and ideological pressures or, in the last case, the sense of anger and desperation and their effect on his action.

   This is encapsulated in the way we choose to describe a man's actions and we can, of course, describe an action in many different ways. Jonathan Glover produced the example of a man who, lost in the desert with some companions, used the last of the drinking water to wash his shirt under the description 'keeping up appearances — even in the desert'. But the choice of description is itself a moral matter. It is already a form of wickedness to describe a suicide bomber as a martyr and not as a murderer of the innocent. Descriptions, as well, may incorporate motives. To call a killer a martyr is to ascribe a motive to him. He killed because he was killing the infidel for the sake of God even at the cost of his own life, something perhaps only possible in an honour culture. (Though there is a tradition in religion, reflected in Eliot's 'Murder in the Cathedral', that martyrdom may be accepted but not sought.) In these ways the choice of a description implies an explanation of the action.

It is a cliché that to understand all is to forgive all. It is fairly obviously untrue, as I have already observed. If we find that a suicide bomber has deliberately targeted a primary school in order to prevent Jewish children growing into adults with a whole life in Israel before them then we will find it very hard to forgive him. It might be less hard if the victims were unselected; the death of those particular individuals would be merely a matter of chance.

'Understanding' carries various shades of meaning and their conflation may have helped to give credence to the idea that to understand is to forgive. 'Being understanding' means being sympathetic. In this case to understand a terrorist involves entering into his motivation in a sympathetic way such that you understand the power of the motives that fuel his action. But, of course, I can understand the ideas and motives which led the Nazis to persecute Jews without in any way endorsing them or sympathising with them. The unconscious or deliberate conflation of these is what leads people to decry attempts to see the reasons behind terrorist actions. I treat the Nazi as rational in the sense that he has reasons for his actions, stupid and wrong-headed as they may be, and I understand the actions of the Palestinian suicide bomber without in any way endorsing them. What he does is wicked. He kills the innocent. He is rational in that his actions derive from beliefs and desires. He is not an automaton. But, in another way, he is irrational. The beliefs of the anti-Semite that Jews are uniquely malevolent and corrupt is stupid and absurd, not least because it treats an entire people as though they were all the same. We operate with two senses of rational, one broader—reflecting the sense in which human beings act in ways which can be explained in terms of their beliefs, and one narrower—the sense in which rational actions are only those based on sensible and sound beliefs which are likely to be effective in achieving the desired outcome.

I have pointed out that to understand is not to extenuate. Indeed it may well have the reverse effect. The action, now understood, turns out to be even worse than we thought. We thought the man killed his wife in a fit of jealous rage and then find out that he had insured her life for a great deal of money in order to be able to live a life of luxury with his mistress. We thought that the murderer killed his victim without prior intention to do so but planned merely to threaten him with a gun in order to get his money. We find out that he killed him because he was Jewish or gay and took the money on impulse. There is no incompatibility at all between declaring an action to be evil and understanding the reasons for it. Indeed, were we to deny that there could be any reasons for a suicide bomber doing what he did, we could not judge him as evil save in the sense that a natural disaster is an evil; the explanations of his behaviour are narrowly causal; he is more of a machine than a man. And in these circumstances, we cannot condemn him without irrationality on our part. He would be no more to be condemned than a hurricane is to be condemned. If we want to describe him as evil we must allow that he acts upon reasons. Human agency involves beliefs, desires, motives and reasons. They can be good or they can be bad. And, of course, social pressure may be such that beliefs cannot be criticised or called into question. Something like this must have been true of the Nazis. A British doctor recalled treating an SS officer in Normandy; he required a blood transfusion; the officer asked whether the British could guarantee that none of the blood had been given by Jews; that could not be guaranteed; the officer refused the transfusion and died. (Those who admire people who act on principle might be impressed by this.) His beliefs were stupid; his idea that Jewish blood is tainted is absurd; we describe it as irrational.

Because of the tendency to distrust explanation as somehow minimising the offence, I have been at pains to show that actions can only be morally evil if they can be explained in familiar human terms, as acts of envy or hatred or as actions brought about by wicked and stupid beliefs. But, turning back to our main interest, forgiveness, we need to recognise that the form of explanation we give of a certain action may sometimes make it easier to see the action in such a context that we can forgive it. Sometimes explanation aids forgiveness, sometimes it does not.

IV

Now one of the many questions begged in the discussion so far is what we can expect in the way of changes to a character. For the possibility of forgiveness may depend upon the extent to which we believe that the offender might have anticipated his offence and might have acted in such a way as to avoid offending. He might simply have placed himself out of the reach of temptation; he might also have embarked on the larger task of changing his character. Equally, for me to forgive may require that I attempt, by judiciously controlling the forms of attention I pay, to change my attitudes. I become more tolerant and less censorious.

But the possibility of such changes is pretty severely circumscribed. How extensive can they be? In some ways it seems easier to change my metaphysics than to change so as to become tolerant of what I currently find intolerable. The questions are very interesting and very general and, in ways I shall pursue, lead to the heart of religious belief. This is not merely because most religions have an interest in moral change. It is more because nearly all religions offer the prospect of survival after death and that must require huge changes.

But let us start at least with less dramatic forms. Could I become an animist or a Parsee? Could I become a Buddhist? This might be easier for me than becoming a Roman Catholic. It is not merely a question of the ontological baggage, the supposed existence of beings about which I am currently sceptical. More to the point are the moral changes required. How could I come to believe that contraception is wrong when I think it is obligatory to use it except when a child is wanted or how could I come to believe that the termination of a pregnancy by a morning-after pill is wrong when it is unthinkable that the fertilised ovum is a human being? What would it be for me to become a Hindu other than to indulge a superficial infatuation with the exotic? My life and my culture are too different. It could be no more than a conceit, a notional option for me.

But many religious traditions believe in the possibility of radical changes. For evangelical Christians the experience of 'being saved' or 'born again' or 'accepting Christ as my Lord and Saviour' are utterly central to the whole business. Without it you are not a Christian, you are not 'saved by grace' and your prospects in the life to come are dismal indeed. So what about a conversion experience? For dramatic changes of this sort are conversions. St Paul became 'a new creature' after his Damascus Road experience. What could this be? A change of character or a change of ideals or both? Can this be a matter of decision? Many Christians believe that it is. If you do make such a 'decision for Christ', to use their terminology, then it will be expected that old ways of behaving will go and new ones will be adopted. The strength to do this is given by God. Such a man may say, in the words of Jesus, that he has been 'born again'. (I believe that George W. Bush and, more surprisingly, Rupert Murdoch, have declared that they are born again, though in the latter case I assume it is a commercial decision.) He might put this metaphorically by saying he is dead to the past; he is a new person. So when the topic of forgiveness comes up I suppose the offender might claim that the offence was committed by his old self (though I have never known anybody do this). The obvious problem with this is that to the extent that the convert is somebody new you are not forgiving *him* but the old personality he has replaced.[12] Still, given that the convert is repentant about his past and never has recourse to this particular form of extenuation, we may place it on one side.

Not many of my readers will have had such opportunities as I had to observe this process of conversion and my own close observation of converts was that, rather than a change of character, it was a replacement of one set of interests with another. They made strenuous and successful efforts to

[12] See Joanna North, 'Wrongdoing and Forgiveness', *Philosophy* 62 (1987), pp 499–508

stop swearing and blaspheming and stopped going to the pictures. Dancing was absolutely out. But squabbling was frequent. The Chapel I attended as a teenager split because the minister did not believe in eternal damnation; he was ousted but meanwhile some of the flock deserted. I imagine they split again because some of them believed that everybody who was not a believer went to Hell, regardless of whether or not they had had a chance to accept the Gospel whilst the others thought that if they hadn't heard, God would not blame them. But that required a sort of limbo which was dangerously close to Papist thinking. Then there were those who believed in predestination and so on. The film 'The Life of Brian' wonderfully pilloried the internecine warfare of splinter groups on the political left but the same pattern is to be found in the cluster of Strict Baptists as opposed to other Baptists, Exclusive Brethren as opposed to common or garden Plymouth Brothers, Primitive versus Wesleyan Methodists, Pentecostalists and the like. The characteristic history of individual converts is rather well exemplified by another anecdote. There was a famous book in the Fifties entitled *I Believed* by a former Communist, Douglas Hyde. From Communism he turned to Catholicism, and one reviewer remarked pertinently that he seemed to have replaced uncritical adherence to one authority with uncritical adherence to another. (The Daily Worker reported this change of allegiance with the observation 'It had been known for some time that he was a Vatican agent'.)

We may admire somebody who, unhappy with the course of her life, elected to change it and changed it by immersing herself in the life of a church. We are certainly encouraged to forgive her her previous offences because she has made an effort to introduce a side to her character which was absent before. There is now more to her than those aspects which brought about her offence. So conversion would be a relevant factor in forgiveness. The question is to what extent it is possible. I have produced some anecdotal evidence to suggest that it is fairly limited.[13] But I am not entirely sceptical. There are no doubt people who have found in religion a cure for the personal antagonisms, the poisoning resentment and quarelsomeness which made life difficult for them and those around them. Unfortunately I have also seen cases of intolerance, censoriousness, backbiting and the baser sorts of politicking amongst new converts.

Concealed here is another complexity. Bernard Williams distinguished between real and notional options, a contrast he attributes to Newman.[14] Thus the life of a Yanomami is not a real option for me. I could live in the jungle and eat what they eat but how could I join in their rituals in the way they do? If they believe in spirits of the forest how could I? I am a product of a western education and life-style. Now bring it closer to home. Could I become a Buddhist? I am inclined to say that I could not. I might subscribe to Buddhist ontologies but the life of a Buddhist set amongst priests and temples in a particular community is not an option for me in Wales. At best I would subscribe to certain beliefs in a Welsh context. After all, I cannot even become a member of a Welsh chapel. Well, you will reply, and rightly, this is all a matter of degree. Of course, I cannot shrug off everything I have learned and absorbed nor can I shrug off my particular heritage but I can change a little or a lot and becoming a Buddhist of a more or less hybrid stamp is one possibility.

What seems likely is that the possibility of such a conversion will become more and more remote the more distant the culture or society. I doubt whether I could become, in any reasonably full sense, a devotee of the cult of Isis. There is then another, more important, question. What sense could I attach to a desire to become a priest of Isis or of Quetzlcoatl? This is relevant because a conversion usually assumes that the individual concerned wants to be con-

---

[13] Classic papers relevant to this are by Bernard Williams, 'Internal and External Reasons' and 'The Truth in Relativism' in his *Moral Luck* (Cambridge University Press, 1981).

[14] Bernard Williams, *Ethics and the Limits of Philosophy* (Fontana, 1985), pp. 160–73.

verted. But the content of a wish or desire may not be clear. Indeed in some cases its intelligibility can be in question. Say a woman wishes to become a Buddhist or perhaps a Roman Catholic. Now the latter might be, perhaps surprisingly, more difficult, in as much as the beliefs we have to subscribe to are more rebarbative for a westerner than the relatively slight demands made upon us by some forms of Buddhism.

Of course, I can persuade myself that I want something without really wanting it. Forms of self-deception are possible in these cases. I might say that I want a particular car. There are no bounds to my imagining what it would be like to have such a car as there might be in trying to imagine becoming a priest of Isis, though I might not have considered the expense involved in running it. There are many degrees of desire. If I were persuaded by somebody else that I need a Jeep then I might end up wanting one, without really wanting it much; I want it in the way that I resignedly take the car to be repaired because it needs the repair even though it is not something I want to do. I might not want to do it because I don't like the business of discussing car problems with mechanics or it might be that I just wish it never went wrong and regard taking it to the garage as a regrettable chore. I might also persuade myself that I want something without knowing much what I am in for. You can raise the enthusiasm of small children for going to the zoo long before they have much idea of what a zoo is like.

The notion of what I want is, as we can see, a complex matter. I can want something very much without having a very good idea of what it would be like to have it. I can want something without knowing that I want it. (Perhaps 'need' would be better here). My wish might be an irrational one in that what I want is very bad for me. Many people seem to want the life of what is called a 'celebrity' without having much idea of the heights of egoism and selfishness involved, the sheer discomfort of a life without privacy and the misery when you are no longer recognised. Conversely I often don't particularly want something when the convenience of having it is something which I have not been able to foresee or imagine. Thus I held out for a long time against buying a mobile phone, partly because I thought them vulgar — only to find that it is extremely useful on the odd occasion.

The end on which I am converging is a discussion of what it would be like to want a heavenly life. People do desire it and I am not suggesting that this is not a genuine wish. What I am suggesting is that it is a wish rather comparable to a small child's wish for an entertainment without much idea of what that entails. For as we extend the notion of a wish for something very remote such as living in a very unfamiliar set of circumstances so we converge on a situation in which the idea of 'wishing for such a state' begins to have some of the vacuity of a small child's desire for an entertainment of which it has no conception.

So is eternal life worth having? This may sound like a silly question. Of course, people will say, it would be better not to die, providing of course, that eternal life did not consist in being roasted in hell. A heavenly life would be certainly better than death at, say, seventy five. Surely it would be preferable if death were not the end. I had better make it clear that I construe heavenly life as believers construe it. After death, the story goes, you wake up again free from pain and discomfort with an eternity to look forward to in the company of those whom you have loved. (What about those who loved you and you could not stand and vice versa?) I am not concerned then with those sophisticates amongst philosophers who interpret eternal life as a change in the quality of this life, on their view it being transparent that the notion of survival of death is foolish even if it were intelligible. This is not what the vast majority of religious people believe and I refuse to patronise them by saying that their ideas are so silly that nobody could possibly believe them.

I shall argue that eternal life is not worth having even if it could be made an intelligible notion. The critical point is that our lives, our decisions, what we value and what we admire is so bound up with our lives on this earth, lives which are limited in length and always at the mercy of accident, that to imagine an utterly different milieu is to imagine a context in which our ordinary wishes, relationships, decisions and preferences become attenuated to the point of extinction.[15]

The imagining of eternal life does not stand isolated. We can imagine other situations which bear more or less closely upon it. We have already considered what is involved in conversion. But there are other, more accessible cases; the thought that life might have turned out differently is easy to grasp. Let's consider some such cases, stages in the progress to endeavouring to imagine something as strange as a life after death. Thus you can imagine some ways in which your life might have been different. 'If only I had set out five minutes later, I would have avoided that awful motor accident'. That is imaginable and presents no great difficulties in conception. You would be somewhat different from the person you are now. You would not have accidentally killed a pedestrian with all that that has entailed for your life even though you were quite innocent. 'If only I had not gone to that party, got drunk and ended in bed with that woman'; the consequences were destructive. It makes rather less sense to me to say 'If only I hadn't read philosophy at university but stayed with English instead'. A philosopher is what I am. Again, supposing I had not taken a post in Wales but stayed in England and taken a post there, then the people I would have met, the strains on my life, the philosophical influences under which I would have come, would have been so different that it begins to seem an idle thought. I really cannot give much content to the sort of person I would now be. Obviously I would still be pursued by the consequences of a fundamentalist Christian upbringing and I would, no doubt, still be interested in music. However I can think more seriously 'If only I had stayed away from school and practised the piano instead'. For then I would be less different from what I am now. After all, there are accidents and accidents. Some speculations are unintelligible;

---

[15] My debt to Bernard Williams is obvious. See his 'The Makropolos Case'; reflections on the tedium of immortality, *Problems of the Self* (Cambridge University Press, 1973).

examples are 'Supposing I had been born into the royal family' or 'Suppose I had been born a Yanomami'. I would not simply be me born to other parents. In this sense there are no accidents of birth.

Here is another series of thought experiments which will take us further on the road towards imagining an eternal life. Would you swap lives with somebody? At what point would the changes imagined be such that you could no longer think of yourself as the same person? At what point would you no longer be able to keep a hold on the thought 'Do I want to be this (or like that)?' At what point does the 'this' begin to affect the 'I' such that the thought-experiment is no longer a possibility?

In some cases I find it hard to distinguish 'Would I want such a life?' from 'Is that life worth living?' For example, if pressed with the question 'Whose life would you rather have, the life of Pope John Paul or the life of Alfred Brendel?', antecedent to confronting the philosophical difficulties, my answer is straightforward. I would rather have had the life of Alfred Brendel. Does that mean 'I would rather have *been* Alfred Brendel'? Well, it might, though that is a thought that makes little sense, as John Locke saw. It might merely mean, as Locke put it, that Brendel ceased to exist and I had a concert career of equivalent celebrity as a classical pianist. Does this mean that I think that Brendel's life is worth living whilst the late Pope's was not? Not necessarily, though in this case I am inclined to think that the life of the late Pope was a life wasted. The issue may come down to the matter of what there was in the late Pope's life which was of value. My own judgement is that the answer is that it was probably not very much since his life was devoted to an illusion and he was complicit in a great deal of human suffering. Implicit in my remarks about the life of a celebrity was that that is a life not worth living. It does not follow that I would rather be dead than be a celebrity, of course. Certainly there are lives which seem to be so bad that one is better off dead; life as a concentration camp guard or prisoner, for example. But it is true that there are lives which seem to be a waste. If the life of Pope John Paul seems to me a life not worth living then, had I been in his position (of course, with my values and attitudes and not his) it only follows that I would have had to change it—not that I would rather be dead. Perhaps there would be some rewards for the daily life without freedom or privacy, a life spent in a grind of administrative detail, services and masses devoted to the glory of a non-existent being. For there might have been some unintended and adventitious side-effects of what was, for him, the main aim in life—that of strengthening the power of the Roman Church. Lives are impoverished to the extent that religion or politics drives out matters of greater significance such as the love of others, the natural world and the arts.

If I think eternal life is not a pleasing prospect, does it follow that I think we should not fear death? Philosophers have debated this over millennia. Since death is extinction, it is argued, there is no reason to fear it. But this is obviously too quick. Fear of death is perhaps natural for a young person. To be deprived of forty years of life, not to be able to see what changes will happen, must be embittering. The changes between the ages of ten and thirty are vast. You find yourself in a career you had not thought of. Never to be given the opportunity to find out such things seems to me dreadful, a reason for sending old men to war rather than the young. But at age seventy, why fear death? I am unconcerned about extinction though I am apprehensive about dying, fearing that it will be protracted and painful. I am afraid of being a coward, of waking up at 3 a.m. and imagining my body cold, inert, wrapped in a sort of nappy. I fear thinking that my wife has a few months to live and then she will no longer be there at my side in bed. I fear the way that those who love the dying man or woman withdraw from him or her, something marvellously caught by Kafka in *Metamorphosis*, immunising themselves from the loss as far as they can. So my fear is not of extinction but of my inability to cope. But that is how I feel now; can I not adjust my fears in the light of what I know to be the case; that if I am old and sick and tired, death seems something to be welcomed, not feared? Montaigne points out that to be very ill is to an extent to relinquish your hold on life; you no longer care so much about survival. The loss of those you love also weakens your desire to live—so that there are many circumstances in which death can seem 'a welcome guest' as Dido's Lament[16] puts it. Weakness and illness become the enemies, not death. No doubt this is so but I find it hard to adjust my present fears in the light of what I can confidently predict. (To feel reasonably fit and know that your death is imminent must be very hard, one reason why capital punishment is indeed 'a cruel and unusual punishment'.)

But even if I believed in some sort of survival after death it would not help to allay the fears of dying. Indeed, in its own right, survival offers nothing very desirable. An utter failure of imagination is characteristic of those who believe in and want a life after death. I am interested here not in the factual question of whether we survive death. I cannot think that we do because, for familiar philosophical reasons, I cannot imagine what would count as such survival. What puzzles me is why it should be thought desirable.

Let me quote a hymn.

> Holy, holy, holy! All the saints adore thee,
> Casting down their golden crowns around the glassy sea;
> Cherubim and Seraphim fall down before thee ...

Brian Morris asked me once, 'What do the saints do after they have cast them down? Pick them up and cast them down again?' I don't think he expected an answer. One might equally wonder whether the Cherubim and Seraphim get up and fall over again. This impoverished vision of what an after-life would be like is extraordinary but entirely characteristic. As I have remarked elsewhere, and I was hardly the first to do so, God must be a bit like the average political leader in his immaturity if he really gets a kick out of this sort of thing. The question on which the remainder of this chapter will turn is: *What would be better than death?*

Now this is not a question which an atheist needs to answer, I suppose, because he probably does believe that

---

[16] In Purcell's *Dido and Aeneas*.

death is complete extinction, though he might use these considerations as a weapon against believers. But for a generous believer who does think that God might find a place for atheists, it is not only a problem for himself but a problem which he faces on behalf of others. It is true that if I don't think a life worth choosing to live, then I might not think an eternal life of the same sort worth choosing to live. But it would not, of course, follow that I would not think it better than extinction. After all, life is the precondition of being able to do anything at all and perhaps we would have the evenings to spare after casting down our golden crowns all day. (Though I suspect that there are no evenings in heaven; there you never get tired and you never want to sleep; but all this is indicative of the trouble one has in conceiving of a heavenly life. A bed is a very attractive proposition when you are tired — and sometimes when you are not tired — Milton's angel blushed when asked whether there was sex in heaven — and replied in the affirmative. Then does anybody in heaven fancy a bit on the side? Do people get jealous? If they don't what does this say about the relationship? Is there wit? Is it sometimes malicious but funny? Do people compose rude limericks? Do people get hungry in heaven? Do they ever have too much to drink and get silly? Will heaven for a petrol head be a matter of Formula One cars being driven around in circles for eternity?)

But the problems go deeper still. In heaven we get all that we wish for (or all that we can, in decency wish for). But for most decent people, self-satisfaction does not count for very much. It plays a minor role indeed, doing what you want is for leisure and for the borrowed moment. A good life involves caring for others, recognising their needs and having things which interest you to the point of absorption, even though they might not interest other people. The pictures we are given of a heavenly life seem to offer little space for this. What can I do to care for somebody all of whose needs are met by Jesus Christ or Allah? The picture of eternal life which is sketched is sufficiently egocentric as to make it puzzling why nice people, and many believers are nice people, would want it. The nadir of this is to be found in those Moslems who believe that martyrs enjoy seventy-seven virgins in paradise (if they really do believe this). The view of women involved is unspeakable. The martyrs might seem more presentable people if their view of paradise was that they offered multiple orgasms to each of seventy-seven women. (I take it that it is seventy-seven virgins and not seventy-seven raisins that are on offer.)

Of course, transmigration of souls does not offer these problems. We come back to a life like this which offers the same sorts of problems and difficulties as those we now face (assuming one comes back as a human being). The impasse here is the unintelligibility of such a proposal. What would count as my being the same person who was born 500 years before me in 1435 as opposed to somebody born in 1436? How would I know such a thing? Suppose I have some memories which seem to be those of a person living in the Tudor period. Would that help? But then how could I distinguish between my remembering these in my own right and my having some mysterious access to the memories of a separate person long dead? All of these hypotheses are of equal implausibility.

There are two subsidiary questions. What would you trade for survival? Would chucking crowns down and picking them up again be worth it? Would perpetual hymn singing? Would you trade the Collected Essays of David Hume for the Collected Sermons of an American TV evangelist like Oral Roberts? Now here is the crunch. Suppose you change so that you come to relish throwing down crowns and picking them up again; suppose it becomes a game of everlasting quoits which you enjoy more than you now enjoy chess. I don't have too much of a problem in imagining this. We can all remember what it was like to be children or teenagers. I well remember a teenager telling me that when he was about eight he thought it would be wonderful to be grown up because then he could buy all the comics he wanted. It did not cross his mind that he would no longer be interested in them. We can all remember the different sorts of things which mattered to us when we were young and how difficult it was to think that one day they would not matter to us. The poor opinion of schoolmates would no longer be of any significance to you. There is also no question but that that child was the same person as you. For here we have physical continuity to guarantee identity. Given that physical continuity may not be on offer, at what point would this cease to be you? Or, if it is still clear that it is you, at what point would you think that survival was not worth the change? Suppose, in twenty years time, through senility, I am reduced to playing pass the parcel in an old people's home; I would think that not worth surviving for even though it would still be me and I might have some memories and powers of recognition. If I feel like this about a passage in my life where there can be no dispute about my identity, how much more would it be so for a heavenly life? The childishness of what is offered in a heavenly life does not seem to me worth the dislocation of survival.

Would life in the Kalahari desert be better than extinction? It would be a life very different from the one I have now and I certainly would not choose it. What means much to me would be lost: the woods, the fields and the coast of Wales, libraries and bookshops and theatre and concerts, but I might very well think it better than some alternatives and better than death. I might very well choose to move to such an area rather than live in a police state but I would still take this life and these interests with me, even if I could not exercise them. What about being released from all desires and merged into the cosmic consciousness, as some Buddhists believe? Far from being better than death that seems to me virtually indistinguishable from it. What about changing to be an animist in the next life, living a life in a forest terrified of ghosts and spirit forces, having no access to books or music? Would that be better than death? Would you choose that as a life after death rather than mere extinction? I certainly do not think it an easy choice.

You will reply, and quite rightly, that it does not have to be like that. The childishness of the hymnal may misrepresent the wonderful things available in another existence. The problem is that although people think they can imagine what heaven is like, they do not try to conceive it in detail.

Far from being a triumph of imagination, it shows a poverty of imagination or, perhaps, a refusal to attempt it.[17]

Again we might consider at what age one is reconstituted. If I were to be resurrected as I am at seventy, it would not be too bad a deal. I am still fit and active though unable to do anything like the amount of physical work I did even ten years ago. O.K. sixty, then? But I would not be able to play squash, which I did enjoy up to the age of fifty and missed when a knee injury forced me to give it up. Fifty then? Well sometimes I remember the pleasure of playing squash but the wish that I could play again is not very strong — nothing like as strong as the desire to play the piano. As you get older your horizons do contract and you may not agonise over-much. But if your interests evaporate utterly is the situation any better than death?

So fifty does not seem a bad age. Yes, but my ideas and interests have changed. I have different ideas about aesthetics to what I then had and different ideas about religion. I am a better pianist and enjoy playing more. Could I have the body of somebody of thirty and my present mind, (if only youth knew, if only age could)? But now we begin to lose contact with what human beings are like. Where the notion of what my capacities, interests and nature are is being stretched to this extent, then it is not just the question of whether it is me that is at issue. That question is, I think, vague and difficult to settle. In some respects it is me and in some respects like me. And some changes may be welcomed. I might wish to be kinder and less interested in competitive sport. The question I raise is whether what is on offer is better than death and, of course, part of that question is whether it is 'really' me that is being preserved. To the extent that I am uncertain about this I might be unready to say that another life is better than death.

So there are limits to what changes can be made to myself such that the outcome is something desirable and these make the prospect of another life less appealing the more fully it is sketched out.

[17] I strongly recommend Michael Frayn's, *Sweet Dreams* (Collins, 1973) as a sardonic and very funny picture of a liberal heaven.

To return, then, to our main topic. If forgiveness requires changes in either the forgiver or the offender, we need to consider whether the changes are intelligible, possible, or desirable. Obviously, we are talking about changes far less extreme than those which occupied our minds in the previous section of this chapter. But they are arguably on a spectrum with the change to another life and changes impose a cost. One convert I knew well maintained that after conversion she was less moody and bad-tempered. Perhaps that was so, though since I did not know her before, I could not tell. But she was certainly very judgemental and censorious of those who lived a different life from her or who espoused different ideas. Edmund Gosse's *Father and Son* gives a wonderful and humourous picture of the milieu. In the hands of such people, forgiveness is a weapon, a means of establishing moral superiority and sometimes the offender will feel that he is better spared it. For conversion does not generally go with the variety of forgiveness I have recommended, benign neglect; rather it is strenuous and involves an attempt to love your enemy. Forgiveness is not, in such cases, an unambiguous virtue.

Chapter Four

Heroes, Villains and Odious Comparisons

But me no buts.

It was a couple of televised interviews that prompted me to raise the questions I want to pose here. I am as often puzzled by what laypeople say as I am by what philosophers say and the best way to start a philosophical discussion has always seemed to me to be a problem. So a half-hearted attempt at analysing what we mean when we say that something is evil will come later instead of at the beginning.

It was suggested on the David Frost TV programme that, when placed besides the evil of the Madrid train bombings, the torture of prisoners at Guantanamo Bay does not amount to very much. And an American lady who infiltrated terrorist networks through the internet and turned them over to the FBI remarked at the end of an interview that, compared with the enormity of 9/11 'a little light torture' is justified. (One wonders what 'a little light torture' amounts to. 'Light torture' suggests parallels with 'light ale'.) Such an argument is not uncommon. This is what I call the 'Yes, but' argument and I find it pretty unsavoury and I suspect that most readers will agree. But what is the rationale behind this misgiving?

Now a principled reply to this might be that our conception of evil is, or ought to be, 'an absolute conception'.[1] I shall take it that this suggests that evils are incommensura-

[1]   Ray Gaita, *Good and Evil. An absolute conception* (MacMillan, 1991). See also Daniel M. Haybron, Moral Monsters and Saints, *Monist* 85 no.2, pp. 260–84.

ble. Evil differs in this from mere wrong-doing, badness or naughtiness of various forms. Acts of evil do not differ in negative value relative one to another. Pressed, we might say that they are all equally evil. By contrast, there is serious badness and there are peccadilloes and we have no problem in comparing these. For example, I don't think that using public money to buy a first class rail ticket for your mistress is anything like as bad as making up a case for war and misleading parliament into supporting it, though it is an interesting reflection on the standards which obtain in British public life that the first is regarded as a resigning matter whilst the second is not. A great deal has been written recently on what is distinctive about evil as opposed to mere badness, and there is a certain plausibility in supposing that what distinguishes evil is its incommensurability, though I have yet to find another author who suggests this. The gist is something like this. To murder an Israeli girl at her twelfth birthday party is evil. To torture Palestinian suspects is evil. The 'Yes, but' argument may be used to say of the second, 'Yes, it is awful but think of the death of the little girl'. The American lady I quoted is saying, in effect, 'Yes, torture is awful, but remember 9/11'. The objection is that these are all awful and we should not grade them. But why should we think that evils are incommensurable?

1. My first thought is that because we cannot measure the sufferings of victims of evil we cannot compare them. There is no metric for suffering. How could we compare the suffering of a woman who knows that in the morning she will be raped by an AIDS-infected gang with that of a man blinded in the Madrid bombing? This does not, I think, move the argument forward. The rhetorical question about a metric for evil merely reasserts the original position, that evils are incommensurable. (You may feel, with justification, that the word 'incommensurable' is not 'le mot juste'. Certainly, there is no metric for acts of heroism any more than there is a metric for acts of evil. But nor is there a metric for more ordinary bad acts or good acts. But 'incomparable,' the obvious alternative, is not a very comfortable fit either, because it tends to carry a positive polarity which we don't

want here. So I stick with 'incommensurable' despite some disadvantages.)

2. Can it be simply a matter of numbers? This, I think, is behind the assumption that the Madrid bombings were worse. Thousands were bereaved and many must have been crippled (we hear little of these). But in Guantanamo Bay it is only the men and their loved ones who are suffering. Where the numbers run into millions, we can no longer grasp such suffering. We cannot grasp the extent of the Holocaust.

But at this point we may be revolted by the thought of making such comparisons and the revulsion is, I think, a moral matter. It would be wrong to make assessments of relative evil.

Somebody might argue that the reason is that the normal processes of explanation and mitigation cannot begin, so that we cannot — on that basis — rate different evils differently. The thought behind this is that some wickedness can be explained by social pressures or through formative events in childhood such that you can come to see why the individual acted as he or she did. Such actions may not be fully under the control of the agent. This is one approach I shall consider later. But, although we may see why a young man whose brothers have been tortured by the Israeli military and whose father has been murdered by settlers may become a suicide bomber, this still does not justify the 'Yes, but' argument. We cannot say 'Yes, torture in Guantanamo Bay is wrong but remember 9/11.' We cannot say 'Yes, it is hard on the Palestinians to bomb their houses and kill their children but look at the suicide bombings' and cannot say either 'Yes, suicide bombings are wrong but look at the deaths of little children at the hands of the Israeli military'.

So if, like me, you find the 'Yes, but' argument objectionable, what explanation would you give? We seem to be locked into a sort of moral absolutism and, perhaps this is right. We ought to say that torture is wrong whatever consequences may flow from it. To argue that information obtained from torture is unreliable is already to have conceded too much.[2] That it is ineffective as a means of obtaining intelligence cannot be the reason for refusing to use it. There is a debate in the USA as to whether torture is justified if it prevents further attacks on American civilians and one defender said it would be *immoral* not to use it. An Australian professor of law recently described torture as 'an excellent information-gathering device'. Such is the pass the 'civilised' west has come to. But I would not be mollified by hearing that the Pentagon had considered using the water torture on Moslem suspects but decided against it on the grounds of its ineffectiveness or because they object to torturing the innocent, something which is virtually inevitable once torture is an option. (We cannot assume that only those who are found guilty will be tortured or threatened with torture in order to elicit further information.) Those who even consider it are already damned as indeed the process of 'extraordinary rendition' already damns them as accomplices in torture.[3]

Now moral incommensurability is not unique to such cases. We do not only find it in the case of evil. The passerby who risks his life by entering a blazing pub to save a child has acted heroically. His action is not less heroic than a similar action which saves two children. Nor is it less heroic than the action of a man who actually dies trying to save a child. These are all heroic actions and they are incommensurable. Such acts, the acts of heroism and saintliness, are called 'acts of supererogation'. To supererogate is 'to do more than is commanded or required' (*OED*, 1971 edn.). Captain Oates was not required to walk into the Antarctic snows to save his comrades; but he did. The young man who lost his life trying to save children in a pub fire in London was not

[2]   Those who advocate torture ought to read. And they might start with Norman Cohn's *Europe's Inner Demons* (Paladin, 1976).

[3]   Common sense tells us that people who are tortured or threatened with torture will, nearly always, confess to what their interrogators require them to confess to. If the natural stupidity of those who defend torture does not enable them to see this, then a cursory reading of a few books on the European witchcraze, or the Stalinist, Maoist and Nazi years will tell them. If these people have not the defence of stupidity or ignorance we can only assume that they are wicked.

obliged to rush into the flames; but he did. To talk of supererogation in this way assumes a framework of obligations
or duties. Thus you are required to look out for the safety of
children in the street but not required to risk your life in sav-
ing them. When you do your action may be praised. You
might even get a medal. So there is customarily not only a
notion of duties in general in the background but, more specifically, a notion of what those duties amount to. The very
etymology suggests it. There will be pretty specific notions
of duty here against which the actions of the saint or hero
are measured. In philosophical parlance, we need a sub-
stantive notion of duty. When we allow this, of course, we
must concede that ideas as to what that duty is may differ.
For ordinary Roman Catholics, there are specific duties
regarding confession and attending Mass as well as requirements which they share with the rest of us. A saint will
spend far more time in the pursuit of these religious duties
than common or garden Catholics. In the nonconformity in
which I was brought up, it was believed that everybody is
called to sainthood, with the consequence that time not
spent in serving the Lord was viewed as time wasted, the
conception of life of which Susan Wolf is eloquently critical
in her essay 'Moral Saints'.[4] Because of the work of Bernard
Williams and others, the notion of a moral saint has seemed
to modern philosophers somewhat disreputable. Saints
have to give up perfectly reasonable and enjoyable
pastimes and they usually become nuisances and pains to
their fellow men. Peter Winch remarked in a paper read at
my university shortly before his death that saints were not
people he cared for and that certainly he would not want to
meet any of them. He did make an exception for Saint Fran-
cis. Many of us would agree. But the notion of a hero has
not, or not yet, received a similar debunking. So heroes may
prove a better basis for a contrast with villains than do
saints. Another advantage is that acts of heroism are almost
always spontaneous. The hero sees a need and acts, sometimes recklessly. We are less enamoured of the saint who

---

[4]   Susan Wolf, 'Moral Saints', often reprinted. See Roger Crisp and
       Michael Slote eds., *Virtue Ethics* (Oxford University Press, 1997).

arranges his or her life to maximise his or her own holiness simply because this can seem self-regarding, though, of course, it need not be so. Equally, of course, we might see a knight errant who goes around seeking damsels in distress so that he can act heroically as a bit of a nuisance and a bore. And we do not need to look further than Don Quixote. But heroes of this sort are antique and we do not need to give them much consideration here.

I said that there needs to be a background of duties against which heroic acts can be measured. Though acts of supererogation are normally discussed in these terms duty is not strictly required. For those who are suspicious of any sort of Kantian ethics, we might be able to get along with a more flexible notion incorporating simply what is customarily expected. It is expected that people will look out for the safety of small children on the street because that is what people care about in a Humean sort of way. Acts of self-sacrifice are special. The second proviso I ought to make is that the acts of self-sacrifice of a hero need to be pretty substantial; they are acts on some sort of scale of sacrifice — and here the notion of commensurability does play a role. Susan Wolf talks helpfully of 'an upper limit' beyond which saintly and, by extension, heroic acts, go. After all, you might forego the largest piece of cake left on the plate because, although you like cake, you know somebody else also likes it. Most of us would do this but such actions would hardly count as supererogatory save in the minimum way. It certainly is not the act of a hero or a saint to leave the largest piece of cake for somebody else. It is more a test of good manners.

Incidentally you can see why supererogation poses a problem for utilitarianism. As a Utilitarian, you are required to maximise the preferences or the happiness of everyone — including yourself. So if I estimate that my taking the biggest piece of chocolate cake will create greater utility than keeping it for others, given that I love chocolate cake more and am rather hungrier than the other guests, then I must eat it. And if we are required to maximise utility, there is no space for saints or heroes; there is no space beyond maximisation. There is just the upper limit and the upper limit is maximisation of utility.

Now what I have been working towards is the suggestion that acts of evil might be acts of negative supererogation. They go beyond what is merely forbidden. To adapt Susan Wolf, they go beyond 'a lower limit' and beyond that lower limit there is no comparing. To compare displays moral insensitivity. Evil is incommensurable. Whether this is a matter of logic, required by the concept of evil, or whether it is merely a matter of moral judgement, I am not sure and although I incline to the latter, I do not have an argument. The clear separation of conceptual and moral considerations is not something I am very confident about.

Negative supererogation seems to fit those cases of evil where pleasure is taken in the wrong-doing. We can imagine that a concentration camp guard might be indifferent to the suffering of the Jews; he has been indoctrinated into thinking that they are sub-human; but he feels guilty about taking pleasure in their suffering. He may not be ashamed of the offence so much as feel uncomfortable about the pleasure he took in it. The harm done is over and above any that might be thought reasonable. Or a policeman may be required to interrogate a subject. This will not be pleasant for the subject. If the policeman gets pleasure from making him squirm or from torturing him so much the worse. Both go beyond what is required in an inverse way to the manner in which a positive act of supererogation such as heroism or self-sacrifice may go beyond what would be normally required. Like acts of heroism in the other direction, nothing requires that such an act of excess cruelty be performed. Corresponding with heroism, as well, it seems to be taking an opportunity to be cruel which has gratuitously offered itself. Taking that opportunity is wicked. But only a few cases of evil are going to answer to the concept of negative supererogation. Obviously a duty-based ethics will reject the notion that we could have negative duties that we might go beyond. But it would also be forced to recognise that some people, in some contexts and cultures, may have a dreadful conception of what their duties are. The Nazi I describe is a case in point and any history of the Middle Ages will list thousands of pious inquisitors whose monstrous behaviour was in answer to duty. In this case, evil amounts to doing one's (misconceived) duty, not going beyond it. But when one goes beyond it one does perform an act of negative supererogation.

It is not an objection that there is no agreement as to what this lower limit is. What is merely a merry jape to one person is cruelty to another. Just as the conception of what our duties consist in may vary, so our conception of what the lower limit is will vary according to our own moral proclivities, background, culture and religion or lack of it. Having said this, I do not want to commit myself to the idea that heroism and utter villainy are symmetrical. I spoke of the actions of the hero as typically impulsive and I think this is more often the case than not — though Captain Oates may have thought over his decision at some length before taking it. But acts of great wickedness are, perhaps, as often planned as not. They say that revenge is a dish best served cold and it may be so. But, as we have seen in an earlier chapter, to maintain the motive for revenge against its gradual fading with the course of time, requires a nurturing of resentment which is deeply unpleasant.

But waiting in the wings is a more serious objection to the incommensurability thesis and it is one discussed by Ray Gaita though he does not seem to see it, as I do, as a problem for an absolute conception of evil. (Indeed I find it difficult to understand what the absolute conception amounts to if this is not a problem for it.) The problem is that we regularly and properly speak of having to choose 'between two evils' or we speak of 'the lesser of two evils'. This certainly suggests that evils are comparable and, were this not the case, the difficulties faced by politicians on a day to day basis would simply not be there. If evils are not commensurable how do we choose between unpalatable alternatives?

In the very considerable recent literature on the concept of evil there seems to be a widespread acceptance that the term is ambiguous or that there are many different sorts of evil. If the evils referred to when we speak of such choices are of a different kind from the evils which are at issue when the 'Yes, but' argument is being aired, perhaps we can make distinctions which will preserve both the rejection of the 'Yes, but' argument and the acceptance that sometimes we have to choose between two evils and that here evils are commensurable. Now traditionally, of course, a distinction is made between moral evils and natural evils. Murder, torture, and imprisonment without trial are instances of the first; they are evils created by mankind. Tsunami, earthquakes and volcanic eruptions which create human suffering are taken to be the latter. The distinction, based as it is on the distinction between natural and human agency, is not entirely perspicuous. In which category should we place the evils committed by a compulsive paedophile whose behaviour has been moulded by childhood abuse? He may not wish to behave this way but he cannot help it.

The distinction has been important in the framing of theodicies, that is, pictures of the cosmos which, while admitting the existence of evil, maintain nonetheless that a benevolent and omnipotent God rules. The creator of a theodicy can concentrate on natural evils if he imagines that moral evils are the consequences of the misuse of the freedom granted to us by God. But note that any theodicy requires evils to be commensurable for it is not compatible with God's nature that He should create and allow the continuing existence of, a universe which has so much evil in it as to outbalance the good. If we demonstrate that some evils are incommensurable then we rob ourselves of a theodicy. For a theodicy the evils cannot be such that no amount of good could compensate for them. Indeed the arguments in Bayle's Dictionary force the author into fideism since he shows that no reasonable account of the existence of evil on such a scale is compatible with God's goodness. The only recourse he has is to accept the revelation of God in scripture and say that his workings are unintelligible to humans. We can give no rational justification for the existence of evil. We can only have faith. One possible line here which has not, as far as I know, been explored, is that the acts of saints and heroes are such that no amount of evil can outweigh them for the simple reason that they cannot be measured. This suggests a more sophisticated theodicy which might make a nice PhD subject (please acknowledge this book). The problem seems to be that evils, being also incommensurable, cannot be outweighed by any amount of good. But perhaps something could be argued here.

Let me return to the case of choosing between evils. The defender of torture will argue as follows. Torture is evil, granted, but the alternative is that we fail to obtain important information, thereby failing to capture terrorists and anticipate their plans. They then kill and maim innocent human beings. Obviously, there are all sorts of things wrong with this argument. First of all, it assumes that the information obtained is accurate. But not many of us are like Jean Moulin in Lyons. Faced with torture we will say anything.[5] Secondly, it assumes the police are torturing the 'right' people i.e. potential or actual terrorists. But this is implausible; it is quite likely they will torture innocent people who either give them useless information or remain silent. If they remain silent it is likely they will be tortured more. Now the opponent of torture might argue at this point that it is worse to have torture going on than to have sporadic outrages killing fifty or so innocent people. They will argue as well that, in the current climate, it will be Islamic young men who are tortured and nothing is more likely to feed terrorism than having your friends and relations tortured whether they are innocent of terrorist plans or not.

The way I have presented the case against torture here will seem to some of you immoral. Basically it is wrong to torture people and there is an end on it, you will say. If you don't regard torture as having an absolute embargo placed upon it, then you are corrupt. I think this objection is correct, as you will already have seen. (I was a little surprised at Gordon Graham's choice of enslaving as a moral absolute

---

[5]   For examples of how people under torture or the threat of torture confess to crimes which are absurd or impossible, see Norman Cohn, *op.cit.* and Glover, *Humanity, op cit.*

i.e. it is such that we cannot conceive of any circumstances which might justify it.)[6]

But there is, in fact, a reply to the accusation that the objections to torture which I list are not moral objections; it is the case that if calculations are being made of what is the lesser of two evils, then we need to take into account consequences and therefore all the considerations I raised against torture are relevant.[7] Furthermore it is a relevant consideration that those who benefit from torture are the innocent people whose lives are saved when terrorist attacks are forestalled. This complicates matters. I can imagine its defenders saying that the torturer, in sacrificing his peace of mind to save others, acts heroically.

Finally, you may argue with Socrates and St. Augustine that it is worse to do evil than to suffer evil and that the torturer harms himself more than his victim. I agree with the first; it is worse to do evil than to suffer evil. But I am more dubious about the second. The consequences to the victim of torture are so grave and permanent that here the Socratic position that the torturer is the more badly harmed seems untenable.

There are, I think, two ways in which we might try to reconcile the fact that we speak of the 'lesser of two evils' with the thesis that evils are incommensurable. The first way is to suggest that the evil we, of necessity, choose is not really evil at all. If the alternative to applying a little light torture, or holding people without charge for ninety days or three years or whatever, is a terrorist outrage, then applying a little light torture or internment is not evil. The American spokesman on Radio Four recently, who argued not only that torture was permissible but that it would be immoral not to use it in the light of the threat posed by terrorism, did not specify which tortures he had in mind. Even wicked men can be quite squeamish about such matters. Himmler

---

[6]   Gordon Graham, *Evil and Christian Ethics* (Cambridge University Press, 2000).

[7]   Susan Neiman remarked somewhere that after Auschwitz nobody could assent to Nietzsche's thesis that what does not kill you makes you stronger.

found it difficult to watch the murder of Jews. If we accept that torture is necessary it is relevant to point out that we will hold that torturing somebody in these circumstances is not evil. An inquisitor who tortured a suspected heretic in order to force repentance would not consider his action to be evil. But this 'solution' suggests sleight of hand. There is no reason to deny that torture in such circumstances is evil. It is.

To take a more plausible case of a choice between evils, few would deny that it would have been right to bomb the concentration camp at Auschwitz in the Second World War. Certainly it would have caused the death of innocent people but they would have died anyway and the destruction of what would nowadays be called a 'facility' would have saved many lives. Nor would anybody deny that this is a case of a choice between two evils. Nevertheless this is, except for a pacifist, the right thing to do. Now the argument might be that since it is the right thing to do it cannot be evil. What would be evil would be to do, deliberately, more than is necessary. And then the notion of negative supererogation comes into play.

This looks intuitively plausible as a way of dealing with this example but it does not do for harder cases.

The second way of dealing with this depends on the contrast I drew between natural and moral evils. A paramedic who was one of the first to reach the victims of the London tube blasts in July 2005 described how he had to make quick decisions as to who could be saved and who must be left to die. But identical decisions must be made when dealing with earthquake victims. Time is short, space and medical supplies are limited and a choice between evils must be made. Now the fact is that the paramedic does not act evilly in making this choice; it is forced upon him and it is forced upon him whether the agency of the disaster is human or natural. The fact that the actions of the suicide bomber are incommensurable in their evil has no bearing upon the paramedic's choice of the lesser of two evils. Whether the suicide bomber kills two or twenty is immaterial in respect to the evil of his action. But post factum, the paramedic finds himself in a position where agency is no longer a relevant consideration. As far as the choices he has to make are concerned, the only way agency could become a factor is if the choices he makes as to who to treat are determined by external considerations; for example, his dislike of a certain race or class of people leads him to treat them last.

This example might suggest an asymmetry between the way we regard future evils and the way we regard past evils. For in this case the evil is already there. It has happened. There are certainly some curious features in parallel; consider pains. For the individual who is going to suffer, pain recalled does not have the same significance as pain anticipated. My attitude to pains I have suffered in the past is that they are now over and done with. I remember them but not even with much of a shudder. Some acute dental pain no longer counts for me as of any significance. I cannot, though, view the suffering of my father in his final illness with the same sort of equanimity. I wish that he had not gone through it and the observation 'it's over now' does not have anything like the same force that it does in the case of my dental pain. Of my father's illness 'It is over' is not dismissive as it is in the case of any pain I have suffered. Of his illness the thought of its being over is that the awfulness has passed and that this is to be counted against the sadness of his death. 'At least he is not suffering anymore' is the thought. This difference between the first person and the third person case does not apply to the future. The prospect of others suffering a painful illness is not to be thought of with equanimity but then neither is the prospect of that happening to me.[8] So we have some sort of precedent for counting differently the future and the past and when we choose between two evils we assume that we are faced with alternatives already set for us either through the evils others have done or through natural evils such as disasters caused by famine, earthquake, accident and the rest.

I conclude then that incommensurability does characterise at least some evil actions; but when we have to choose

---

[8]   I have been helped by discussing this with David Cockburn.

between two evils, then they are commensurable; for the agent it is a matter of indifference whether these are moral or natural evils and natural evils are commensurable. An earthquake which kills a hundred is worse than an earthquake which kills two. It does not matter to the paramedic's decision whether the explosion on the tube was caused by a suicide bomber or somebody carrying home an abnormally large quantity of fireworks for Guy Fawkes night.

Hold on, you will say, but what about the hard cases I described? Are they not still hard cases which I have done nothing to deal with? Supposing somebody is forced to choose between using torture to elicit valuable information and risking a terror outrage, however implausible this scenario may be?[9] Are they not forced to choose and do they not choose the lesser of the two evils? My answer to this is to focus on the concept of choice here. Suppose you could provide an example, a case where a terrorist is known to be guilty and is suspected of having information about further outrages. Suppose too, less plausibly still, that no amount of questioning will get it out of him. We are left with two alternatives; more innocent deaths or torture. Both are evil. I maintain that these evils are incommensurable and that the dilemma here is that no moral choice can be made; this is just why these are very hard cases. We can opt for one alternative or the other but opting is not, in one sense of 'choosing', choosing. Plumping is not choosing in the sense of being a reasoned decision. There are cases where we cannot choose between evils in the full sense of choosing, that is in a reasoned and morally defensible way. There are no reasons which could be given which outweigh the fact that torture is evil.

From acorns do mighty oaks grow. For my conclusions are firstly, as you will already have gathered, that a

---

[9]   It is odd that philosophers are accused of inventing preposterous examples as though they alone are guilty of this. On the BBC Radio Four programme, 'The Moral Maze', Melanie Phillips presented the lawyer Michael Mansfield with a theoretical choice between imprisoning a man known to be innocent and a terrorist bombing in central London. He reasonably enough refused to answer on the grounds that the two are unconnected.

theodicy is an impossibility, and secondly, that a principled ethical theory offering solutions to all the moral dilemmas we may find ourselves in is also an impossibility. Ethics, as David Cockburn once said to me, is a mess. But it is, I think, a natural born mess. Of its nature there will be hard cases and insoluble dilemmas.

II

We must now return to our main theme. Are acts of evil also distinguished by being unforgivable? Indeed are there unforgivable offences? Christian theology tends to say that there are not, save in the rather curious case of a sin against the Holy Ghost. Matthew 12, 31–2. (Why the Holy Ghost in particular rather than the rest of the Trinity?) In fact the question is ambiguous. Is the impossibility of forgiving supposed to be psychological or logical? If forgiveness is necessarily a matter of conquering resentment then it might well be psychological. It is not achieved until resentment is overcome and that can be hard and involve a struggle with one's predilections. In a particular case the offended may find it impossible to offer a complete reconciliation with the offender; he simply cannot conquer the resentment he feels and there is no forgiveness. This assumes that it is the full Christian sense of forgiveness that is in question; it is in that sense of forgiveness that forgiveness is impossible here. But suppose we take another form of forgiveness. If forgiveness was ever merely a speech act then an investigation into the conditions under which it was possible might be an investigation into the conditions in which it made sense to utter the words 'I forgive you'. Then, I think, whether or not there are unforgivable sins would probably be a matter of logic, widely construed. We would have to consider the circumstances in which one could sensibly say 'I forgive you'.

Set these questions aside for the moment. It is perhaps natural to look for cases of what is unforgivable in those actions which are evil, though there may be cases where an action is not forgivable because one of the parties has died. (This does point up the gravity of murder. You kill the one person who is in the prime situation to forgive.) So let us consider some possibilities.

An offence might be unforgivable when it is utterly inexcusable. That is, the normal processes of extenuation, of seeing that the offender has more to herself than those features which led to the offence, somehow make no difference. The offence is so awful that nothing can be done about it. Think of a case like that described in *Sophie's Choice*. A mother is told to choose between her children. One will be saved, the other will go to the gas chamber; if she does not make a choice both will die. Whatever decision she makes she will live with it. The evil-doer has put her in a position which will leave her with a sense of irreparable guilt for the rest of her life. This is a calculated stratagem to ruin the woman's life. Suppose we learn, as well might be the case, that there is another side to the offender; away from the concentration camp he is a decent family man and loves animals. Suppose he later feels terrible remorse. None of this will ameliorate the situation. As Hannah Arendt observed, these actions are beyond forgiveness and beyond punishment. Nothing we can do to the perpetrator is proportional to the offence. In such a case Christian forgiveness might be psychologically impossible; there is nothing she can conceivably learn about the offender which can place his actions in a light which makes possible the sort of extenuation or understanding required for forgiveness. And in such a case the impossibility is surely not just a matter of individual psychology. If she did forgive him, we might question whether she really had and if she had indeed, we might condemn her forgiveness as irrational. We might indeed feel that about the vicar who forgave the man who raped his daughter or the minister who forgave the IRA terrorists who murdered his daughter. In a previous chapter I described how Ivan in *The Brothers Karamazov* presents his brother Alyosha with a story of a landowner who murdered a serf boy who had committed a trivial offence. Ivan continues

> … what's the good of avenging them, what's the good of consigning their murderers to hell, what good can hell do when the children have already been tortured to death?

> And how can harmony exist if hell exists too? I want for-
> giveness, I want to embrace everyone, I want an end to suf-
> fering. And if the suffering of children is required to make
> up the total suffering necessary to attain the truth, then I
> say here that no truth is worth such a price. And above all, I
> don't want the mother to embrace the torturer whose dogs
> tore her son apart! She has no right to forgive him! Let her,
> if she will, forgive him her own suffering, her own extreme
> anguish as a mother but she has no right to forgive the suf-
> fering of her mutilated child; even if the child himself
> forgives, she has no right.

Could unforgivable actions be actions which are unintelligible? Then the strongest case for unforgivability will
perhaps be made; depending on how we understand
'unintelligible', it may be that the impossibility is a logical
matter. If an evil action is unforgivable (in the richer sense of
'forgive') because there is nothing which can be a reason for
it, then the impossibility of forgiveness will be a logical one
because the action cannot be understood and if it cannot be
understood then the normal processes which lead to forgiveness in its richer sense cannot begin. Now there is what
analytic philosophers would call a research project, the origins of which are to be found in Hannah Arendt's thought
that, in the face of the holocaust, those of us who are atheists
need to find a secular conception of evil, a notion of evil that
will not carry the implication of Satanic forces at work.[10]
Arendt's suggestion was that an evil action is one that 'cannot be deduced from humanly explicable notions'. It is, to
that extent, unintelligible. (Arendt's other famous observation concerned the banality of evil but this seems to have
been anticipated; it is expressed by implication in the night-
mare Ivan suffers in *The Brothers Karamazov* when he meets
the Devil [Book 11, chapter 9]. The Devil is shabby, dressed
in faded and worn clothes which are rather out of fashion.
'In short he was a picture of impecunious respectability'. He
has 'that air of self-importance typical of the true parasite,
eager to be obliging and conciliatory from the start'.)

---

[10] See Gordon Graham, *Evil and Christian Ethics* (Cambridge University Press, 2000), on whether a secular conception is possible.

Now I have heard a case made out not only for regarding the actions, say, of Nazi concentration camp guards as unintelligible but, further, that it is important that they should be seen as such. Thus, you might think that the murder of a child is a sort of limit. We want to say that it is impossible though not in the sense that it cannot be done. The murder of a child is an extreme example but there are others of a contrived type familiar to philosophers. Your grandmother has only days to live. Would you kill her, painlessly, for a million pounds? I can imagine somebody saying 'this is something I simply cannot do' and so it cannot enter into the terms of argument. Of course, in a sense, I can do it. There is an axe in the shed. Get it and bring the sharp end heavily down on her head. But there is also a sense in which I cannot do it. It is outside my range. I can imagine somebody thinking they can do it and then abandoning the attempt when it comes to it. When Utilitarians ask you whether it would not be right to kill your grandmother if the alternative was a terrorist bombing of Oxford Street, then what they invite you to do is to place in the argument a consideration which lies beyond the limit of possible action. In fact, a Utilitarian begins, on this account, to resemble a sociopath. In order to achieve an end, he contemplates or acts on, considerations which the rest of us simply do not countenance. And torture should be one such. The difference is in the ends which prompt the Utilitarian to act. Mr Hyde, R.L. Stevenson's picture of a sociopath, bumped into a child at a corner and 'trampled calmly over the child's body and left her screaming on the ground'. She was in his way, and he trod on her. But the Utilitarian's considerations are somewhat loftier. Still, what the Utilitarian asks us to do is what I declared, in the first part of this chapter, to be impossible — to choose, on grounds and therefore with reason, between killing one's grandmother and allowing a terrorist outrage. I do not think that such a choice or, more plausibly, Sophie's choice, can be thought of as a reasoned choosing of one alternative over the other. And if you think that it is then I suggest you concentrate for a moment on the detail of the action. Your grandmother is lying in bed. She says 'Good morning dear' whereupon you produce the axe from behind your back and smash her skull, scattering blood and brains all over the sheets. Go on! Think it through! I assume that you and any other reader would be paralysed by the prospect and unable to do it. At least I hope so. The casual cruelty of the concentration camp guard whose action may be a species of negative supererogation is an action that some would describe, I think, as inexplicable.

In fact there are three other ways in which understanding evil may present problems. Suppose understanding evil involves putting oneself in the position of the person who did it; one can imagine rebelling against such a process. To identify with the perpetrator runs the risk of becoming more like him and that is a risk too far. Secondly the process of understanding may involve my saying 'I could have done that too, had I been in his position'. This we might not want to contemplate. The fear of imagination corrupting the personality lies behind our reservations on both these matters. Perhaps, though, we should resist this latter. Andrew Gleeson[11] points out that recognising our common vulnerability to evil is important in humanising evil-doers and, in this, he is surely right. The British gutter press routinely demonises evil-doers and, deliberately, underwrites the response of its readers. 'Yes, I may be bad-tempered at home, sometimes dishonest and sometimes violent, but at least I am not a child-molester or somebody who beats up old ladies'. ('I thank God I am not as other men are.') But I cannot be sure that, had I been subject to the pressures that the Hitler Youth were under, I might not have become a concentration camp guard or, had I been sexually abused as a child, I might not have ended up as a child molester. Few of us know our breaking points and what histories might have been possible for us. The third consideration presses less upon us and Gleeson's approach suggests why we should reject it; the suggestion is that an imaginative identification with evil doers ends up with our hating the perpetrators or their actions less than we currently do or perhaps

[11] *Humanising Evil-Doers.*

should. Of course, the orthodox reply to the third consideration is to distinguish between the sin and the sinner — though this in itself harbours some difficulties which we have already addressed. After all, what a man is is, to at least some extent, what he does. In the previous chapter we saw how this separation between sin and sinner may be accomplished. But we ought not to minimise either the risks or the difficulties of it. You cannot easily bracket off what he does as 'not the real him' and when we do this we do so in somewhat restricted circumstances and generally with an ulterior motive, sometimes laudable in the case of others, less so when it is our own action we are downgrading.

On any account which stresses their unintelligibility, evil actions, which lie beyond what we can contemplate as moral human beings, are actions which necessarily cannot be approached using the 'external' techniques to accelerate forgiveness which I described earlier. We cannot view such an evil-doer as less than free in the way I have described; the problem is more basic; he is not just under the sway of ideas which have been drummed into him; we cannot see that he has reasons at all which could explain his doing what he did. Some readers might very well place a suicide bomber in this category.

I have to say that I am not convinced by all this, partly for considerations I share with Gleeson. The effect of upbringing, an ideology or religion which precludes criticism and inquiry, together with the pressure to conform, can make monsters of most of us. Indeed I find it less hard to imagine that somebody might, in extremis, do such a wicked thing than I can imagine the murders involved in, say, the rape of Nanking and these are, after all, explicable.

It has been suggested that the evil-doer silences the considerations against the act. They are not simply outweighed. They have been put out of court altogether. It would remain to be settled whether actions which are unforgivable overlap with actions which are evil or whether one is a sub-class of the other. The thought must be that the deliberate stifling of reservations makes it hard to extenuate and thus hard to forgive. The absence of a conscience might be understood as a result of childhood abuse or something similar but the deliberate placing of the conscience out of court altogether is much worse. But there seems an element of stipulation in such an analysis simply because many agents perform evil actions by allowing other considerations to outweigh those which militate against them without stilling the voice of conscience altogether. Macbeth and Raskolnikov in Dostoevsky's *Crime and Punishment* offer examples.[12]

Let me draw some conclusions. I am inclined to reject the generalisation that evil actions are, in general, unintelligible. Some may be and it is important for our understanding of evil and forgiveness that this is so; but we can find all sorts of reasons why an SS man ill-treated the Jews; he was brought up to regard them as sub-human and a danger to mankind. Given the circumstances it was extremely difficult for him to challenge these ideas. As Richard Norman points out, there is a sort of partial altruism going on here.[13] Loyalty to the group matters so much that it enables the committing of crimes required by the group. Indeed, it seems to me likely that evil behaviour is more commonly a result of the exchange of one set of social mores for another than the traditional conception which takes evil behaviour to involve the surrender of the reason before the passions, a view common to Platonic and Christian theorising. The idea there is that we somehow revert to the state of animals, a state of nature in which rapine and murder is the norm though nobody who knows much about social animals would regard this as bestial conduct. That would be unfair to animals.

It is then less difficult to see the evil of ethnic cleansing as something inexplicable; we may even see how somebody comes to cancel the normal human resistance to hurting small children. We explain but in no way mitigate. Likewise to say that an act is done out of envy, resentment or malice explains but might not mitigate, though once we start to

---

[12]   See Geoffrey Scarre, *After Evil* (Ashgate, 2004), and Eve Garrard, 'The nature of Evil', *Philosophical Explorations*, 1 (1998), pp. 43–60.

[13]   Richard Norman *On Humanism* (Routledge, 2004), p. 117.

enquire into why the agent is envious or malicious, matters will probably become more complicated. Samuel Johnson thought that envy was the worst of sins since it sought no good for itself. But one can think of ways in which mitigation is possible. Somebody who is insecure and has low self-esteem may very well resent those who are more successful. Once again though, such a move treats the offender as less fully an agent. Again I do not suggest that he is completely lacking responsibility. What we are inclined to think, looking at the pressures upon him and taking into account his history, is that it would be hard for him to behave otherwise.

To summarise. An action which is evil must be, I suggest, first a great crime. It involves very serious harm to others. I don't think that anything in particular is gained by using the notion of an atrocity such as an act of terror as a paradigm.[14] There are acts of evil which affect only one individual. A single case of torture is evil but not an atrocity. An act of terror is an evil and I define an act of terror as an act calculated to achieve political ends by the harming of the innocent. The bombing of the World Trade Centre in 2001 was probably an act of terror; it certainly was an act of great evil. The bombing of British cities by the Luftwaffe and the bombing of Dresden and Hamburg by the British were acts of terror.

Although I have suggested that it is not the case that evil acts are necessarily unforgivable, I do suggest that an evil action is often unforgivable in the rich sense. They are in many ways the paradigm of the unforgivable. Take a final example. In 1992, Governor Clinton, as he then was, broke off his Presidential Campaign to return to Alabama to sign the death warrant for a mentally ill prisoner. I do think this was an evil thing to do though Clinton may not be an evil man. Nevertheless Clinton did it, I assume, in full knowledge of the situation and he did it knowing that to be soft on the death penalty would spell doom for his election chances. He did not deceive himself about the mental condi-

[14] See Claudia Card, *The Atrocity Paradigm* (Oxford University Press, 2002).

tion of the condemned man nor was it a case where his moral principles temporarily gave way, something which did happen from time to time.

I have made two large claims:

a) Evils are incommensurable in a way that other crimes, misdemeanours and natural disasters are not.

b) Since a theodicy requires such comparisons, theodicies can be ruled out. They are not merely inadequate to the task of reconciling the goodness of God with the existence of Evil. They are morally abhorrent — and here I register my support for D.Z. Phillips in his lifelong battle against such theodicies. His moral outrage is entirely justified.

III

The issues that arise with the concept of forgiveness thus have their parallels in the concept of evil. We are led to think that what is evil is unforgivable, for the normal procedures which lead to explanation and, sometimes extenuation, often, though not inevitably, prove impossible. Certainly the way the concept is used suggests as much. It is effectively an argument terminator. Once something or somebody has been declared evil, it is assumed that we can forego the normal processes of understanding. I have expressed reservations about this. Whatever your conclusions about this issue, there still remains a way in which any action can be forgivable. Forgiveness in the sense of wishing no further harm to befall the offender is possible. In this thinner sense, forgiveness is always possible.

Epilogue

I end with a fictional example chosen because it reveals the extent to which we are concerned with ideas whose limits and applicability are so vague and ill defined that it is really hard to know what we should say. These concepts are liquid.

The example is from a novel by Charles Morgan, *The River Line*.[1] Morgan is a once-celebrated novelist who has fallen out of favour. Unlike, say, Joyce Cary, the neglect is justified. As you will see from my synopsis, Morgan is a novelist rather akin to Sartre; one always has the suspicion that his characters dance according to his pre-ordained concerns; the corresponding strength is that his novel does have some of the force of Greek tragedy. He is a philosophical novelist in the same way and it is not surprising that his reputation is higher in France than here. The portentousness of his style probably appeals to the French intelligentsia as well. Nevertheless, *The River Line* is an interesting novel for a philosopher to read and it exemplifies a number of moral issues with insight. I am afraid that giving a synopsis takes some of the steam out of reading it but that is unavoidable if I am to discuss it here. The 'River line' is an 'underground railroad' in occupied France moving Allied pilots and agents through a series of safe houses to the Spanish border. It is clearly crucial that it not be infiltrated by what were called 'faux Anglais' who would reveal its existence to the Gestapo. The story concerns a group of four, three Englishmen and one American; it is from the American's point of view that the story is told; he reveals a Jamesian contrast

---

[1] The novel was brought to my attention by Michael McGhee.

between American optimism and European experience. One Englishman is fluent in French and German and frequently chats with Germans in the streets. The American, Sturges, notices a letter to Leipzig in his pocket just before they reach the border. He alerts their French agent, Marie, who orders an English officer Wystantly, to kill him which he does, immediately. After the war and Marie's release from Ravensbruck, Wystantly marries Marie and they settle in the Cotswolds where they are visited by Sturges who falls in love with an English girl. With a contrivance at which even Dickens or Hardy might have baulked, the girl proves to be the sister of the murdered Englishman who was, in fact, a bona fide airforce officer.

Now the dilemma for Sturges is apparent. He cannot marry and keep his wife ignorant of the fact that he was instrumental in the killing of the brother to whom she was deeply attached. But to tell her, when he thinks she assumes her brother died in combat, would be to place a burden on her which would be unreasonable. Wystantly also knows the truth but never told Marie and the circumstances show why. She returned from the concentration camp very ill and her slow recovery gave the relationship a chance to grow without there being an opportunity to speak. I think Morgan makes a subtle point here. You cannot build a relationship on a lie but there may be cases where you cannot yourself responsibly tell the individual concerned for reasons to do with her (or his) well-being. Later it may be too late. But then, relationships always throw up the problem of how much, or how little, to say. In fact the girl twigs and Sturges can begin a relationship with her.

But, of course, this is by no means an optimistic ending. The protagonists live with the fact that they have, in ignorance, done something terrible. They carry the weight of a terrible mistake and it is no comfort to say that a hard decision was made in good faith.

Two features of the novel interest me. Does the girl, Valerie, forgive Sturges? If she does, she does so without, it seems, first passing through the stage of resenting him. Is the fact that she reminds Sturges so strongly of her brother in any way related to the possibility of reconciliation, if reconciliation is what is happening? What we have is a situation where a discovery might have been expected to terminate a relationship but it does not. What Valerie does might well be described as forgiving the protagonists. Is there a thought that she is sufficiently similar to count as a surrogate? Valerie is so close to and so similar to her brother that she might be thought to be an acceptable substitute - somebody who now can do the forgiving.

And, in a way, since he is dead, she is the only one in a position to do so. But the latter consideration is not the former. Were it only that Valerie was in the same position as Senator Wilson, the surviving victim of the IRA atrocity, the one who has been damaged, it would not matter that she was similar to or particularly close to her brother. She would still be the victim. Her similarity suggests something more, that she can forgive on his behalf, for he, had he survived, would have done so. Admittedly, all this presumes that forgiveness is a relevant consideration and you might think that, although they are right to feel that their lives have been irrevocably damaged by a mistake made in good faith, forgiveness simply does not arise any more than it can for those Oedipus has injured in ignorance.

Bibliography

Arendt, Hannah (1974), *The Human Condition* (University of Chicago).

Augustine, St. *Confessions*, trans. Pine-Coffin (Penguin).

Benn, Piers (1996), 'Forgiveness and Loyalty', *Philosophy* 71: 369–83.

Bennett, Christopher (2003),'Personal and Redemptive Forgiveness', *European Journal of Philosophy*, 11, 127–44.

Berlin, Isaiah (1997), 'The Pursuit of the Ideal', in *The Proper Study of Mankind* (Chatto and Windus).

Braithwaite, R.B. (1955), *An Empiricist's View of the Nature of Religious Belief* (Cambridge University Press).

Burrow, J.W. (2000), *The Crisis of Reason* (Yale).

Butler, Joseph : 'Upon Forgiveness of Injuries,' *Sermon IX*.

Calhoun, Cheshire (1992),'Changing One's Heart,' *Ethics* 103, 76–96.

Card, Claudia (2002), *The Atrocity Paradigm; A Theory of Evil* (Oxford University Press).

Care, Norman S. (1996), *Living With One's Past* (Rowan and Littlefield, Lanham MD).

Cohn, Norman (1970), *Pursuit of the Millennium* (Paladin).

Cohn, Norman (1976), *Europe's Inner Demons* (Paladin).

Cupitt, Don (1994), *The Sea of Faith* (SCM).

Dostoevsky, Fyodor (1994), *The Karamazov Brothers*, trans. Ignat Avsey (Oxford University Press).

Downie, R.S. (1965),'Forgiveness,' *Philosophical Quarterly* 15 128–34.

Flanagan, O. and Rorty, A.O. eds.(1990), *Identity, Character and Morality: Essays in Moral Psychology* (MIT, Bradford).

Frankfurt, Harry G. (1988), *The Importance of What We Care About* (Cambridge University Press).

Frankfurt, Harry G. (2004), *The Reasons of Love* (Princeton University Press).

Frayn, Michael (1973), *Sweet Dreams* (Collins).

Gaita, Raymond (1991), *Good and Evil; An Absolute Conception* (MacMillan).

Garrard, Eve and McNaughton, David, (2002),'In Defence of Unconditional Forgiveness,' *Proc. Aristotelean Society* vol. 103; 39–60.

Gleeson, Andrew (2006), 'Humanizing Evil-Doers,' in *Judging and Understanding: Essays on Free Will, Justice, Forgiveness and Love*, Pedro Tabensky ed. (Ashgate, Aldershot).

Glover, Jonathan (2001), *Humanity, a Moral History of the Twentieth Century* (Pimlico).

Govier, Trudy (1999),'Forgiveness and the Unforgiveable,' *American Philosophical Qtly*, 36; 59–75.

Govier, Trudy (2002), *Forgiveness and Revenge* (Routledge).

Graham, Gordon (2000), *Evil and Christian Ethics* (Cambridge University Press).

Hare, R.M. (1998), *Essays on Religion and Education* (Clarendon Press).

Harman, Gilbert (1999), 'Moral Philosophy Meets Social Psychology': Virtue Ethics and the Fundamental Attribution Error, *Proceedings Aristotelean Society*, Vol. XCIX, pp. 315-31.

Harvey, Jean(1993), 'Forgiving as an Obligation of the Moral Life,' *Int. Journal of Moral and Social Studies*, 8, pp. 211–22.

Haybron, Daniel M (1999), 'Evil Character,' *American Philosophical Quarterly*, 36, pp. 131–48.

Holloway, Richard (2002), *On Forgivenes* (Canongate).

Holmgren, Margaret (1993), 'Forgiveness and the Intrinsic Value of Persons', *American Philosophical Qtly*, 30, pp. 341–52.

Horsbrugh, H.J.N. (1974/5), 'Forgiveness,' *Canadian Journal of Philosophy*, 4, pp. 269–82.

Hughes, Paul M. (1993), 'What is Involved in Forgiving', *Journal of Value Enquiry*, 27, pp. 331-40.

Hughes, Paul M.(1994), 'On Forgiving Oneself'; a reply to Snow, *Journal of Value Enquiry*, 28, pp. 557–60.

Hughes, Paul M.(1997), 'What is Involved in Forgiving,' *Philosophia*, vol. 25, pp. 33–49.

Hursthouse, Rosalind (1987), *Beginning Lives* (Blackwell).

Kekes, John (1990), *Facing Evil* (Princeton University Press).

(1993), *The Morality of Pluralism* (Princeton University Press).

Kolnai, Aurel (1977), 'Forgiveness', in *Ethics, Value and Reality* (Athlone).

Korsgaard, Christine M (1996), *The Sources of Normativity* (Cambridge University Press)

Lang, Berel (1994), 'Forgiveness' *American Phil. Qtly.* 30.

Lewis, Meirlys (1980), 'On Forgiveness', *Philosophical Quarterly*, 30, pp. 236–45.

McGinn, Colin (1997), *Ethics, Evil and Fiction* (Oxford University Press).

Mackintosh, H.R. (1927), *The Christian Experience of Forgiveness* (Nisbet, London).

Milo, Ronald (1984), *Immorality* (Princeton).

Minas, Anne C. (1975), 'God and Forgiveness', *Philosophical Quarterly* 25, pp. 138–50.

Montaigne, Michel de (2003), *The Complete Essays*, trans. M.A. Screech (Penguin).

Murphy, Jeffrie G. and Hampton, Jean (1988), *Forgiveness and Mercy* (Cambridge University Press).

Neblett, W.R. (1974), 'Forgiveness and Ideals', *Mind*, 83, pp. 269–75.

Neiman, Susan (2004), *Evil in Modern Thought* (Princeton University Press).

Norman,Richard (2004), *On Humanism* (Routledge).

North, Joanna (1987), 'Wrongdoing and Forgiveness', *Philosophy*, 62, pp. 499–508.

O'Shaughnessy, R.J. (1987), 'Forgiveness', *Philosophy*, 42, pp. 336–52.

Patton, John (1985), *Is Human Forgiveness Possible?* (Abingdon Press, Nashville).

Phillips, D.Z. (2004),*The Problem of Evil and the Problem of God* (SCM).

Proust, Marcel (1989), Swann's Way (Overture), in *Remembrance of Things Past*, trans. C.K. Scott Moncrieff and Terence Kilmartin (Penguin).

Quinn, Philip, L. (1986), 'Christian Atonement and Kantian Justification', *Faith and Philosophy*, 3; 4, pp. 440–62.

Richards, Norvin (1988), 'Forgiveness', *Ethics*, 99.

Roberts, Robert C. (1995), 'Forgivingness', *American Phil. Qtly.*, 32, pp. 289–306.

Rorty, R. (1999), *Philosophy and Social Hope* (Pelican Books, Harmondsworth).

Ross, Lee and Nisbett, Richard E. (1991), *The Person and the Situation; Perspectives of Social Psychology* (Temple University, Philadelphia).

Sandel, M.J. (1981), *Liberalism and the Limits of Justice* (Cambridge University Press).

Scarre, Geoffrey (2004), *After Evil; Responding to Wrongdoing* (Ashgate, Aldershot).

Sharpe, R.A. (1990) *Making the Human Mind* (Routledge, London).

Sharpe, R.A. (1992), 'Moral Tales', *Philosophy*.

Sharpe, R.A. (1996), 'Character, Conversion and Identity,' in K.S. Johanessen and T. Nordenstam eds., *Wittgenstein and the Philosophy of Culture* (Holder-Pichler-Tempsky); The Proceedings of the 1995 Wittgenstein Symposium in Kirchberg, pp. 232–43.

Sharpe, R.A. (1997), *The Moral Case Against Religious Belief* (SCM Press, London).

Snow, Nancy (1993), 'Self-forgiveness', *Journal of Value Inquiry*, 27, pp. 75–80.

Taylor, Gabriele (1985), *Pride, Shame and Guilt* (Oxford University Press).

Williams, Bernard (1973), *Problems of the Self* (Cambridge University Press).

Williams, Bernard (1981), *Moral Luck* (Cambridge University Press).

Williams, Bernard (1985), *Ethics and the Limits of Philosophy* (Fontana).

Wolf, Susan (1997), 'Moral Saints', often reprinted. See Roger Crisp and Michael Slote eds., *Virtue Ethics* (Oxford University Press).

Woodruff, Paul (2001), *Reverence* (Oxford).

SOCIETAS

essays in political and cultural criticism

Societas: Essays in Political and Cultural Criticism

Public debate has been impoverished by two competing trends. On the one hand the trivialization of the media means that in-depth commentary has given way to the ten-second soundbite. On the other hand the explosion of knowledge has increased specialization, and academic discourse is no longer comprehensible.

This was not always so, especially for political debate, but in recent years the tradition of the political pamphlet has declined, as publishers found that short books were uneconomic. However the introduction of the digital press makes it possible to re-create a more exciting age of publishing. *Societas* authors are all experts in their own field, but these accessible essays are written for a general audience.

The books are available retail at the price of £8.95/$17.90 from your local bookshop, or using the order form in the main Imprint Academic catalogue, or online at imprint-academic.com/books. However you can obtain the current volume on bi-monthly subscription for £5/$10 (back volumes only **£2.50** each for new subscribers), using the Direct Debit form on the back cover of this pamphlet. Details and updates at **imprint-academic.com/societas**

The Right Road to Radical Freedom

Tibor R. Machan

The Right Road to Radical Freedom

Tibor R. Machan

This work focuses on the topic of freedom. The author starts with the old issue of free will – do we as individual human beings choose our conduct, at least partly independently, freely? He comes down on the side of libertarians who answer Yes, and scorns the compatibilism of philosophers like Daniel Dennett, who try to rescue some kind of freedom from a physically determined universe. From here he moves on to apply his belief in radical freedom to areas of life such as religion, politics, and morality, tackling subjects as diverse as taxation, private property, justice and the welfare state.

Tibor Machan is no mere theoretician. He was smuggled out of Hungary in 1953, as a 14-year old, and served in the US Air Force before taking up academic life. He has written many books and presents his robust views in a trenchant no-nonsense style. The author teaches ethics at Chapman University and is a research fellow at Stanford University's Hoover Institution.

128 pp., £8.95/$17.90, 9781845400187 (pbk.), January 2007, *Societas*, Vol.26

Paradoxes of Power: Reflections on the Thatcher Interlude

Sir Alfred Sherman (1919-2006)

Thumb through the index of any study of the Thatcher years and you will come across the name of Sir Alfred Sherman. In her memoirs Lady Thatcher herself pays tribute to his 'brilliance', the 'force and clarity of his mind', his 'breadth of reading and his skills as a ruthless polemicist'. She credits him with a central role in her achievements.

Born in 1919 in London's East End, until 1948 Sherman was a Communist and fought in the Spanish Civil War. But he ended up a free-market crusader. Sherman examines the origins and development of 'Thatcherism', but concludes that it was an 'interlude' and that the post-war consensus remains largely unscathed.

'These reflections by Thatcherism's inventor are necessary reading.' **Sir John Hoskyns**, *Salisbury Review*
'This book should be read by anyone examining this period.' **Margaret Thatcher**
'These essays are highly relevant to the politics of today.' **Norman Tebbit**
'Sherman suplied much of the drive to turn back the tide of collectivism.' *Guardian*
'Sherman made a crucial and beneficient contribution to modern Britain.' *Independent*

edited by Mark Garnett, University of Lancaster
200 pp., £8.95/$17.90, 9781845400927 (pbk.), March 2007, *Societas,* Vol.27

Public Health & Globalisation

by Iain Brassington

This book claims that the NHS is morally indefensible. There is a good moral case in favour of a *public* health service, but these arguments do not point towards a *national* health service, but to something that looks far more like a *transnational* health service.

Drawing on Peter Singer's famous arguments in favour of a duty of rescue, the author, who lectures in law at Manchester University argues that the cost of the NHS is unjustifiable. If we accept a duty to save lives when the required sacrifice is small, then we ought also to accept sacrifices in the NHS in favour of foreign aid. This does not imply that the NHS is wrong; just that it is hard to justify speding thousands of pounds on one person in Britain when the money could save many more lives elsewhere.

96 pp., £8.95/$17.90, 9781845400798 (pbk.), May 2007, *Societas,* Vol.28

Why Spirituality is Difficult for Westerners

David Hay

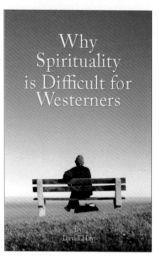

A zoologist by profession, David Hay holds that religious or spiritual awareness is biologically natural to the human species and has been selected for in organic evolution because it has survival value. Although naturalistic, this hypothesis is not intended to be reductionist with regard to religion. Indeed, it implies that all people, even those who profess no religious belief, nonetheless have a spiritual life.

This book documents the repudiation of religion in the West, describes the historical and economic context of European secularism, and considers recent developments in our understanding of the neurophysiology of the brain as it relates to religious experience.

Dr Hay is Honorary Senior Research Fellow at the University of Aberdeen.

96 pp., £8.95/$17.90, 9781845400484 (pbk.), July 2007, *Societas,* Vol.29

Earthy Realism: The Meaning of GAIA

Mary Midgley (ed.), James Lovelock (foreword)

GAIA, named after the ancient Greek mother-goddess, is the notion that the Earth and the life on it form an active, self-maintaining whole. By its use of personification it attacks the view that the physical world is inert and lifeless.

It has a *scientific* side, as shown by the new university departments of earth science which bring biology and geology together to study the continuity of the cycle. It also has a visionary or *spiritual* aspect. What the contributors to this book believe is needed is to bring these two angles together. With global warming now an accepted fact, the lessons of GAIA have never been more relevant and urgent.

Contributors include James Lovelock, Mary Midgley, Richard Betts, Susan Canney, Maggie Gee, Brian Goodwin, Stephan Harding, John Mead, David Midgley, Anne Primavesi, Joan Solomon, Pat Spallone, John Turnbull, David Wilkinson and John Ziman.

Mary Midgley is a philosopher with an interest in relations between humans and the rest of nature (especially animals), in the sources of morality, and in the tendency of 'scientism' to become a religion.

120 pp., £8.95/$17.90, 9781845400804 (pbk.), Sept. 2007, *Societas,* Vol.30

Joseph Conrad Today

Kieron O'Hara

This book argues that the novelist Joseph Conrad's work speaks directly to us in a way that none of his contemporaries can. Conrad's scepticism, pessimism, emphasis on the importance and fragility of community, and the difficulties of escaping our history are important tools for understanding the political world in which we live. He is prepared to face a future where progress is not inevitable, where actions have unintended consequences, and where we cannot know the contexts in which we act.

Heart of Darkness uncovers the rotten core of the Eurocentric myth of imperialism as a way of bringing enlightenment to 'native peoples' – lessons which are relevant once more as the Iraq debacle has undermined the claims of liberal democracy to universal significance.

The result can hardly be called a political programme, but Conrad's work is clearly suggestive of a sceptical conservatism of the sort described by the author in his 2005 book *After Blair: Conservatism Beyond Thatcher*. The difficult part of a Conradian philosophy is the profundity of his pessimism – far greater than Oakeshott, with whom Conrad does share some similarities (though closer to a conservative politician like Salisbury). Conrad's work poses the question of how far we as a society are prepared to face the consequences of our ignorance.

96 pp., £8.95/$17.90, 9781845400668 (pbk.), Nov. 2007, *Societas,* Vol.31

Who Holds the Moral High Ground?

Colin J Beckley and Elspeth Waters

Meta-ethical attempts to define concepts such as 'goodness', 'right and wrong', 'ought' and 'ought not', have proved largely futile, even over-ambitious. Morality, it is argued, should therefore be directed primarily at the reduction of suffering, principally because the latter is more easily recognisable and accords with an objective view and requirements of the human condition. All traditional and contemporary perspectives are without suitable criteria for evaluating moral dilemmas and without such guidance we face the potent threat of sliding to a destructive moral nihilism. This book presents a possible set of defining characteristics for the foundation of future moral evaluations and engagements, taking into consideration that the historically maligned female gender may be better disposed to ethical leadership.

96 pp., £8.95/$17.90, 9781845401030 (pbk.), January 2008, *Societas,* Vol.32

Froude Today

John Coleman

A.L. Rowse called fellow-historian James Anthony Froude the 'last great Victorian awaiting revival'. The question of power is the problem that perplexes every age: in his historical works Froude examined how it applied to the Tudor period, and defended Carlyle against the charge that he held the doctrine that 'Might is Right'.

Froude applied his analysis of power to the political classes of his own time and that is why his writings are just as relevant today. The historian and the prophet look into the inner meaning of events – and that is precisely what Froude did – and so are able to make judgments which apply to ages far beyond their own. The last chapters imagine what Froude would have said had he been here today.

120 pp., £8.95/$17.90, 9781845401047 (pbk.), March 2008, *Societas,* Vol.33

The Enemies of Progress

Austin Williams

This polemical book examines the concept of sustainability and presents a critical exploration of its all-pervasive influence on society, arguing that sustainability, manifested in several guises, represents a pernicious and corrosive doctrine that has survived primarily because there seems to be no alternative to its canon: in effect, its bi-partisan appeal has depressed critical engagement and neutered politics.

It is a malign philosophy of misanthropy, low aspirations and restraint. This book argues for a destruction of the mantra of sustainability, removing its unthinking status as orthodoxy, and for the reinstatement of the notions of development, progress, experimentation and ambition in its place.

Al Gore insists that the 'debate is over'. while musician K.T. Tunstall, spokesperson for 'Global Cool', a campaign to get stars to minimize their carbon footprint, says 'so many people are getting involved that it is becoming really quite uncool *not* to be involved'. This book will say that it might not be cool, but it is imperative to argue against the moralizing of politics so that we can start to unpick the contemporary world of restrictive, sustainable practices.

The author is the director of the Future Cities Project and tutor at the Royal College of Art and Bartlett School of Architecture and the Built Environment.

96 pp., £8.95/$17.90, 9781845400989 (pbk.), May 2008, *Societas,* Vol.34

Debating Humanism

Dolan Cummings (ed.)

More than to sleep and feed, to be human is to debate, to argue and to engage with the ideas and opinions of others. And a recurring theme is the very question of what it means to be human, and the nature of our relationship to the world, to each other and to gods or God. This has never been an idle debate: it is intimately bound up with how society is organised and where authority lies. Broadly speaking, the humanist tradition is one in which it is we as human beings who decide for ourselves what is best for us, and are responsible for shaping our own societies. For humanists, then, debate is all the more important, not least at a time when there is much discussion about the unexpected return of religion as a political force determining how we should live.

This collection of essays follows the Institute of Ideas' inaugural Battle of Ideas festival at the Royal College of Art in London in October 2005. Contributors include Josie Appleton, Simon Blackburn, Robert Brecher, Andrew Copson, Dylan Evans, Revd. Anthony Freeman, Frank Furedi, A.C. Grayling, Dennis Hayes, Elisabeth Lasch-Quinn, Kenan Malik and Daphne Patai.

96 pp., £8.95 / $17.90, 9781845400699 (pbk.), *Societas,* Vol.25

Village Democracy

John Papworth

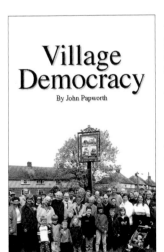

'A civilisation that genuinely reflects all that human beings long for and aspire to can only be created on the basis of each person's freely acknowledged power to decide on each of the many questions that affect his life.' In the forty years since he wrote those words in the first issue of his journal *Resurgence*, John Papworth has not wavered from that belief. This latest book passionately restates his argument for radical decentralisation as the only answer to the current crises in politics, trade, ecology and international affairs.

Revd. John Papworth is founding editor of *Resurgence* and *Fourth World Review*. His many books including *Small Is Powerful*.

'If we are to stand any chance of surviving we need to heed Papworth's call for decentralisation'
Zac Goldsmith, *The Ecologist*

'If anything will save this world and in time enough, it will be the insightfulness and wisdom John Papworth displays in this little volume.' **Kirkpatrick Sale**

96 pp., £8.95 / $17.90, 9781845400644 (pbk.), *Societas,* Vol.24

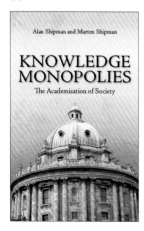

Knowledge Monopolies
Alan Shipman & Marten Shipman

Historians and sociologists chart the *consequences* of the expansion of knowledge; philosophers of science examine the *causes*. This book bridges the gap. The focus is on the paradox whereby, as the general public becomes better educated to live and work with knowledge, the 'academy' increases its intellectual distance, so that the nature of reality becomes more rather than less obscure.

'A deep and searching look at the successes and failures of higher education.' *Commonwealth Lawyer*

'A must read.' *Public* (The Guardian)

£8.95/$17.90, 9781845400286 (pbk), *Societas* V.20

The Referendum Roundabout
Kieron O'Hara

A lively and sharp critique of the role of the referendum in modern British politics. The 1975 vote on Europe is the lens to focus the subject, and the controversy over the referendum on the European constitution is also in the author's sights.

The author is a senior research fellow at the University of Southampton and author of *Plato and the Internet, Trust: From Socrates to Spin* and *After Blair: Conservatism Beyond Thatcher* (2005).

£8.95/$17.90, 9781845400408 (pbk), *Societas* V.21

The Moral Mind
Henry Haslam

The reality and validity of the moral sense took a battering in the last century. Materialist trends in philosophy, the decline in religious faith, and a loosening of traditional moral constraints added up to a shift in public attitudes, leaving many people aware of a questioning of moral claims and uneasy with a world that has no place for the morality. Haslam shows how important the moral sense is to the human personality and exposes the weakness in much current thinking that suggests otherwise.

'Marking a true advance in the discussion of evolutionary explanations of morality, this book is highly recommended for all collections.'
David Gordon, *Library Journal*

'An extremely sensible little book. It says things that are really rather obvious, but which have somehow got forgotten.' **Mary Midgley**

£8.95/$17.90, 9781845400163 (pbk), *Societas* V.22

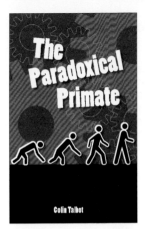

The Paradoxical Primate
Colin Talbot

This book seeks to explain how human beings can be so malleable, yet have an inherited set of instincts. When E.O. Wilson's *Consilience* made a plea for greater integration, it was assumed that the traffic would be from physical to human science. Talbot reverses this assumption and reviews some of the most innovative developments in evolutionary psychology, ethology and behavioural genetics.

'Talbot's ambition is admirable…a framework that can simultaneously encompass individualism and concern for collective wellbeing.' *Public* (The Guardian)

£8.95/$17.90, 9780907845850 (pbk), *Societas* V.14

Putting Morality Back Into Politics
Richard D. Ryder

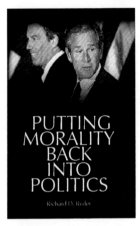

Ryder argues that the time has come for public policies to be seen to be based upon moral objectives. Politicians should be expected routinely to justify their policies with open moral argument. In Part I, Ryder sketches an overview of contemporary political philosophy as it relates to the moral basis for politics, and Part 2 suggests a way of putting morality back into politics, along with a clearer emphasis upon scientific evidence.

Trained as a psychologist, Ryder has also been a political lobbyist, mostly in relation to animal welfare.

£8.95/$17.90, 9781845400477 (pbk), *Societas* V.23

Tony Blair and the Ideal Type
J.H. Grainger

The 'ideal type' is Max Weber's hypothetical leading democratic politician, whom the author finds realized in Tony Blair. He is a politician emerging from no obvious mould, treading no well-beaten path to high office, and having few affinities of tone, character or style with his predecessors. He is the Outsider or Intruder, not belonging to the 'given' of British politics and dedicated to its transformation. (The principles outlined are also applicable. across the parties, in the post-Blair period.) The author was reader in political science at the Australian National University and is the author of *Character and Style in English Politics* (CUP).

'A brilliant essay.' **Simon Jenkins**, *Sunday Times*
'A scintillating case of the higher rudeness.' *Guardian*

£8.95/$17.90, 9781845400248 (pbk), *Societas* V.15

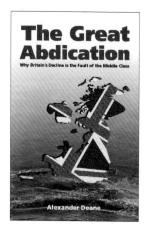

The Great Abdication
Alex Deane

According to Deane, Britain's middle class has abstained from its responsibility to uphold societal values, resulting in the collapse of our society's norms and standards. The middle classes must reinstate themselves as arbiters of morality, be unafraid to judge their fellow men, and follow through with the condemnation that follows when individuals sin against common values.

> '[Deane] thinks there is still an element in the population which has traditional middle-class values. Well, maybe.' **George Wedd**, *Contemporary Review*

£8.95/$17.90, 9780907845973 (pbk), *Societas* V.16

Who's Afraid of a European Constitution?
Neil MacCormick

Neil MacCormick

Who's Afraid of a European Constitution?

This book discusses how the EU Constitution was drafted, whether it promises any enhancement of democracy in the EU, whether it implies that the EU is becoming a superstate, and whether it will strengthen the principle of subsidiarity and the protection of human rights.

Sir Neil MacCormick is professor of public law at Edinburgh University. He was an MEP and a member of the Convention on the Future of Europe.

> 'Those with a passing curiosity should find [the book] informative. Those already familiar... should find it entertaining and thought provoking.' *Scolag Legal J.*

£8.95/$17.90, 9781845392 (pbk), *Societas* V.17

Darwinian Conservatism
Larry Arnhart

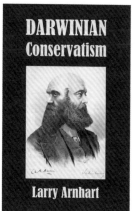

DARWINIAN Conservatism

Larry Arnhart

The Left has traditionally assumed that human nature is so malleable, so perfectible, that it can be shaped in almost any direction. Conservatives object, arguing that social order arises not from rational planning but from the spontaneous order of instincts and habits. Darwinian biology sustains conservative social thought by showing how the human capacity for spontaneous order arises from social instincts and a moral sense shaped by natural selection. The author is professor of political science at Northern Illinois University.

> 'Strongly recommended.' *Salisbury Review*
> 'An excellent book.' **Anthony Flew**, *Right Now!*
> 'Conservative critics of Darwin ignore Arnhart at their own peril.' *Review of Politics*

96 pp., £8.95/$17.90, 9780907845997 (pbk), *Societas*, Vol. 18

The Last Prime Minister
Graham Allen MP

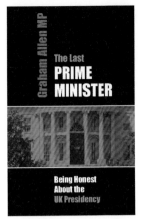

This book shows how Britain has acquired an executive presidency by stealth. It is the first ever attempt to codify the Prime Minister's powers, many hidden in the mysteries of the royal prerogative. This timely second edition takes in new issues, including Parliament's impotence over Iraq.

'Iconoclastic, stimulating and well-argued.' **Vernon Bogdanor**, *Times Higher Education Supplement*

'Well-informed and truly alarming.' **Peter Hennessy**

'Should be read by anybody interested in the constitution.' **Anthony King**

£8.95/$17.90, 9780907845416 (pbk), *Societas* V.4

Doing Less With Less: Britain More Secure
Paul Robinson

Notwithstanding the rhetoric of the 'war on terror', the world is now a far safer place. However, armed forces designed for the Cold War encourage global interference through pre-emption and other forms of military interventionism. We would be safer with less. The author, an ex-army officer, is assistant director of the Centre for Security Studies at Hull University.

'Robinson's criticisms need to be answered.'
Tim Garden, *RUSI Journal*

'The arguments in this thesis are important and should be acknowledged by the MOD.'
Major General (Retd.) Patrick Cordingley DSO

£8.95/$17.90, 9781845400422 (pbk), *Societas* V.19

The Snake that Swallowed its Tail
Mark Garnett

Liberal values are the hallmark of a civilised society, but depend on an optimistic view of the human condition, Stripped of this essential ingredient, liberalism has become a hollow abstraction. Tracing its effects through the media, politics and the public services, the book argues that hollowed-out liberalism has helped to produce our present discontent. Garnett is the co-author of *The Essential A-Z Guide to Modern British History*.

'This arresting account will be read with profit by anyone interested in the role of ideas in politics.'
John Gray, *New Statesman*

'A spirited polemic addressing the malaise of British politics.' **Michael Freeden**, *The European Legacy*

£8.95/$17.90, 9780907845881 (pbk), *Societas* V.12

The Party's Over
Keith Sutherland

This book questions the role of the party in the post-ideological age and concludes that government ministers should be appointed by headhunters and held to account by a parliament selected by lot.

'Sutherland's model of citizen's juries ought to have much greater appeal to progressive Britain.' *Observer*

'An extremely valuable contribution.' *Tribune*

'A political essay in the best tradition – shrewd, erudite, polemical, partisan, mischievous and highly topical.' *Contemporary Political Theory*

£8.95/$17.90, 9780907845515 (pbk), *Societas* V.10

Democracy, Fascism & the New World Order
Ivo Mosley

Growing up as the grandson of Sir Oswald, the 1930s blackshirt leader, made Ivo Mosley consider fascism with a deep and acutely personal interest. Whereas conventional wisdom sets up democracy and fascism as opposites, to ancient political theorists democracy had an innate tendency to lead to extreme populist government, and provided unscrupulous demagogues with the ideal opportunity to seize power. In *Democracy, Fascism and the New World Order* Mosley argues that totalitarian regimes may well be the logical outcome of unfettered mass democracy.

'Brings a passionate reasoning to the analysis'. *Daily Mail*

£8.95/$17.90, 9780907845645 (pbk), *Societas* V.6

The Case Against the Democratic State
Gordon Graham

This essay contends that the gross imbalance of power in the modern state is in need of justification and that democracy simply masks this need with the illusion of popular sovereignty. The book points out the emptiness of slogans like 'power to the people', as individual votes do not affect the outcome of elections, but concludes that democracy can contribute to civic education.

'Challenges the reigning orthodoxy'. *Mises Review*

'Political philosophy in the best analytic tradition… scholarly, clear, and it does not require a professional philosopher to understand it' *Philosophy Now*

'An excellent candidate for inclusion on an undergraduate syllabus.' *Independent Review*

£8.95/$17.90, 9780907845386 (pbk), *Societas* V.3

Off With Their Wigs!
Charles Banner and Alexander Deane

On June 12, 2003, a press release concerning a Cabinet reshuffle declared as a footnote that the ancient office of Lord Chancellor was to be abolished and that a new supreme court would replace the House of Lords as the highest appeal court. This book critically analyses the Government's proposals and looks at the various alternative models for appointing judges and for a new court of final appeal.

'A cogently argued critique.' *Commonwealth Lawyer*

£8.95/$17.90, 9780907845843 (pbk), *Societas* V.7

Universities: The Recovery of an Idea
Gordon Graham

Research assessment exercises, teaching quality assessment, line management, student course evaluation, modularization, student fees – these are all names of innovations in modern British universities. How far do they constitute a significant departure from traditional academic concerns? Using some themes of J.H. Newman's classic *The Idea of a University* as a springboard, this book aims to address these questions.

'Those who care about universities should thank Gordon Graham.' **Anthony O'Hear**, *Philosophy*

'Deserves to be widely read.' *Political Studies Review*

'It is extraordinary how much Graham has managed to say (and so well) in a short book.' **Alasdair MacIntyre**

136 pp. *Societas*, Vol.1, subscription (retail edn: 9781845401009, £14.95/$29.90)

The Liberty Option
Tibor R. Machan

The Liberty Option advances the idea that it is the society organised on classical liberal principles that serves justice best, leads to prosperity and encourages the greatest measure of individual virtue. The book contrasts this Lockean ideal with the various statist alternatives, defends it against its communitarian critics and lays out some of its more significant policy implications. The author teaches ethics at Chapman University. His books on classical liberal theory include *Classical Individualism* (Routledge, 1998).

'The arguments are anchored largely in American politics, but have a wider resonance. A good read.' *Commonwealth Lawyer*

£8.95/$17.90, 9780907845638 (pbk), *Societas* V.5

Self and Society
William Irwin Thompson

The book is a series of essays on the evolution of
culture, dealing with topics including the city and
consciousness, evolution of the afterlife, literary and
mathematical archetypes, machine consciousness
and the implications of 9/11 and the invasion of Iraq
for the development of planetary culture. The
author is a poet, cultural historian and founder of
the Lindisfarne Association. His sixteen books
include *Coming into Being: Artifacts and Texts in
the Evolution of Consciousness.*

£8.95/$17.90, 9780907845829 (pbk), *Societas* V.9

The Modernisation Imperative
Bruce Charlton & Peter Andras

Modernisation gets a bad press in the UK, and is
blamed for increasing materialism, moral
fragmentation, the dumbing-down of public life,
declining educational standards, occupational
insecurity and rampant managerialism. But
modernisation is preferable to the likely alternative
of lapsing back towards a 'medieval' world of static,
hierarchical and coercive societies – the many and
serious criticisms of modernisation should be seen
as specific problems relating to a process that is
broadly beneficial for most of the people, most of
the time.

'A powerful and new analysis'. **Matt Ridley**

£8.95/$17.90, 9780907845522 (pbk), *Societas* V.8

Why the Mind is Not a Computer
Raymond Tallis

The equation 'Mind = Machine' is false. This pocket
lexicon of 'neuromythology' shows why. Taking a
series of keywords such as calculation, language,
information and memory, Professor Tallis shows
how their misuse has a misled a generation. First of
all these words were used literally in the description
of the human mind. Then computer scientists
applied them metaphorically to the workings of
machines. And finally the use of the terms was
called as evidence of artificial intelligence in
machines *and* the computational nature of thought.

'A splendid exception to the helpless specialisation
of our age' **Mary Midgley**, *THES*
'A work of radical clarity.' *J. Consciousness Studies*

£8.95/$17.90, 9780907845942 (pbk), *Societas* V.13

Our Last Great Illusion
Rob Weatherill

This book aims to refute, primarily through the prism of modern psychoanalysis and postmodern theory, the notion of a return to nature, to holism, or to a pre-Cartesian ideal of harmony and integration. Far from helping people, therapy culture's utopian solutions may be a cynical distraction, creating delusions of hope. Yet solutions proliferate in the free market; this is why therapy is our last great illusion. The author is a psychoanalytic psychotherapist and lecturer, Trinity College, Dublin.

'Challenging, but well worth the engagement.' *Network*

£8.95/$17.90, 9780907845959 (pbk), *Societas* V.11

God in Us: A Case for Christian Humanism
Anthony Freeman

God In Us is a radical representation of the Christian faith for the 21st century. Following the example of the Old Testament prophets and the first-century Christians it overturns received ideas about God. God is not an invisible person 'out there' somewhere, but lives in the human heart and mind as 'the sum of all our values and ideals' guiding and inspiring our lives.

The Revd. Anthony Freeman was dismissed from his parish for publishing this book, but remains a priest in the Church of England.

'Brilliantly lucid.' *Philosophy Now*
'A brave and very well-written book' *The Freethinker*

£8.95/$17.90, 9780907845171 (pbk), *Societas* V.2

Societas: Essays in Political and Cultural Criticism

The books in this pamphlet are available retail at the price of £8.95/$17.90 from your local bookshop, or using the order form in the main Imprint Academic catalogue, or online at **imprint-academic.com/books**. See also our larger catalogue of monographs, collected essays and periodicals in philosophy, politics, psychology and cultural and religious studies.

However you can obtain the current volume (and back issues) on bi-monthly subscription for only £5/$10, using the direct debit form on the back of this brochure. Updates at **imprint-academic.com/societas** (overseas readers can subscribe via our credit card direct debit scheme.)

IMPRINT ACADEMIC, PO Box 200, Exeter, EX5 5HY, UK
Tel: (0)1392 851550   Fax: (0)1392 851178   sandra@imprint.co.uk

Cover painting: 'The Tryst' by John B. Harris

To qualify for the Direct Debit subscription rate, we will debit your account £5.00/$10.00 when each new book is despatched (every two months). We will supply you with details of the next title at the same time, so if you want to unsubscribe you can cancel the mandate at any time.

☐ Please register my *Societas* subscription, starting with the current title (see month of publication on p. 2–6 or at **imprint-academic.com/societas**). I would also like to order the following backlist titles for **only £2.50/$5.00 each.**

. . . .

. . . .

. . . .

IMPRINT ACADEMIC

Please fill in the form and send to
Imprint Academic, PO Box 200,
Exeter EX5 5YX

**Instruction to your Bank or
Building Society to pay by Direct Debit**

DIRECT Debit

To: The Manager   Bank/Building Society

Address

                                              Postcode

Name(s) of Account Holder(s)

Branch Sort Code

Bank/Building Society account number

Originator's Identification Number

| 6 | 3 | 0 | 4 | 9 | 4 |

Reference

Instruction to your Bank or Building Society

Please pay Imprint Academic Direct Debits from the account detailed in this Instruction subject to the safeguards assured by the Direct Debit Guarantee. I understand that this instruction may remain with Imprint Academic and, if so, details will be passed electronically to my Bank/Building Society.

Signature(s)

Date

DD15

Banks and Building Societies may not accept Direct Debit Instructions for some types of account

Name. . . . .

Address * . . . .

Home telephone . . . . E-mail. . . . .

Send completed form to Imprint Academic, PO Box 200, Exeter EX5 5HY, UK